NO TENSION

ONE MAN'S INCARCERATION WITHIN THE INDIAN PRISON SYSTEM

By

Barry Hulse

Acknowledgements

I wish to express my gratitude to all the wonderful people who believed in me and deemed me worthy of being capable of sharing my stories with the world. I would also like to thank all the people who wrote to me and helped me through the ordeal—you know who you are.

Dedication

This book is dedicated to my late mum, who sadly passed away in November 2022 before I could publish it!
Without her continuous letters, visits, and fight to get me home, I possibly would not be here to tell my tale today.

I love you, Mum, rest in peace, sleep tight.

Contents

Chapter One

The entirety of eternity is available at this point. We catch everlasting time through our creative imagination. We can never recover lost time. Memory enables us to taste the glittering experience of living by recalling our past in a progression of successive events and happenings. Composing our own story calls for us to recall the impression of what it involves to live by an illusion of tangibility before losing the clarity of the brain. Everything in the world can be recovered but not time. The pendulum of time is not in our control; the time I spent away is still lost. No matter what I do, it stays lost.

On 21st Nov 2009, my life took an unexpected turn. What had started as a usual morning became the most dreaded moment of my life. From sips of tea to thoughts of what'll happen next, it was as if I had been sent into someone's worst nightmare. It was certainly not mine, though, partly because I had never imagined something like this would ever cease to exist in my life. And, while I waited for it to be over soon, I 1realised it was just the beginning, the beginning of the worst chapter of my life.

Every part of my life has always been ordinary, but even amidst our ordinary, busy, and sometimes messy day-to-day lives, there is so much beauty and grace if we keep an eye out for it.

I had my people beside me, I had everything I wanted, family, friends, and a routine, and I was travelling just like I typically did, the usual basic norm that almost every one of us believes in. But, on 21st Nov 2009, everything but normal happened.

'Life is what happens to us while we are making other plans'.

—Allen Saunders

I packed my bags and set off from Manchester to Goa for a one-week vacation like I always did. Goa, for me, was a perfect destination to take a break from our routine life. Its beaches and festivals always amazed me. I had been there many times before, but it was never enough. However, this time, I wished I had never been there in the first place.

I had no clue that the next few moments would have a severe impact on a huge part of my life, the after-effects of which would last a lifetime. Life is so unpredictable; you walk straight into the worst chapter of your life without you even knowing it.

After years of agony, torment, and anguish, I have finally come to a point in life where I just want it to end. I lost a precious time of my life to something that wasn't even supposed to be, to begin with. It's been a while now, but it still feels like yesterday. Every night I go to bed contemplating every 'what if' I can think of. I think it's about time I allow myself some closure. I need this, and I certainly deserve this.

Life isn't easy, and it certainly isn't easy when you're forced to spend a part of your life reaping for what someone else sows. People might forget what happened, but they can never forget how it made them feel, and to this day, it haunts me.

I gave in an enormous amount of emotion, effort, and struggle to injustice, patience, and torture, and even though it has physically ended, there's this ongoing misery that still holds me back. Throughout those years, I came across people from different walks of life and learnt some of the basic lessons of life the hard way.

Before it all happened, I was a completely different person. My routine included parties and befriending new people. I was already working in a well-reputed firm. My son loved me, and my mum and I were still best friends. At that moment, if I had a choice to go back in time and change anything, I wouldn't think twice before entering it all over again. I loved everything about it. For me, seeing was believing. I mean, I knew bad things happen and that there are bad people out there. But they were certainly nowhere near me. I was living the life I wanted and dreaming big.

Due to that incident, not only did I lose time, I lost the person I used to be. Something inside me had crushed. It wasn't instant. I assure you of that. It was as if the fire inside me had been put out. It was as if someone had stepped upon a blooming flower, but it was a gradual process. The time came and took the best of me with it.

I no longer consider myself an extrovert. Parties and crowds no longer excite me. I look for peace and solace. I look for a time when I can have a moment to myself and relax. Wounds heal, but the scars remain. They last longer than we'd imagine.

Sometimes, they're a reminder of how you struggled, and sometimes, they're a reminder of how you survived.

Some nights, you go back in time wishing how what happened never did. Then, you snap back to reality. You did go through all that torment. All that misery of trying to get back to your family, all that pain of fighting to prove your innocence, all that anguish of just trying to pass through time, moment by moment, not knowing what and how far the end may be, waiting for a moment that might not even come. Imagining and building up scenarios in your head of reuniting with your loved ones.

My life doesn't just revolve around misfortune; my life stands on the grounds of trust, betrayal, and survival.

Friendship, to me, is never giving up. It has no boundaries, and it has no rules. Friendship is the purest form of trust. There's really no point in taking a leap of faith in friendships. Friends aren't supposed to break your heart; friends are supposed to be your support system, the ones you reach out to in times of trouble.

However, friends do end up breaking your heart, and this is probably the most underestimated kind of heartbreak. My friend didn't just break my trust, he snatched my life, and he broke the ground I walked on.

'Stab the body, and it heals, but injure the heart, and the wound lasts a lifetime'.

—Mineko Iwasaki

Actually, things went south long before the 21st of November 2009 arrived. I just wasn't aware of it. A storm was coming, and I was as calm as the summer sea.

Who would have imagined something so brutal and evil would be an outcome of something so naïve, so pure?

That is how I was. I was straightforward and simple with everyone, so I expected the same in return.

Unfortunately, life isn't fair. And you mostly never receive what you give—what means the world to you might not even exist for someone else.

Whether it was my trust in him that brought to me the darkest moments of my life or it was his betrayal that cost me more than I could afford, I served time for a crime I did not commit and that, to this date, sends shivers down my spine. Yes!

On 21st November 2009, I was arrested. The people who were waiting to receive me at the Dabolim Airport were customs officers from Mumbai. The moment they received me was the very moment everything I valued and believed in started to come crashing down. It was a sudden hit, believe me. It came out of nowhere and shook the very core of my soul.

'There is a feeling of disbelief that comes over you, that takes over, and you kind of go through the motions. You do what you're supposed to do, but in fact, you're not there at all'.

—Frederick Barthelme

My name had appeared on the computer screen with a LOC (look out circular), and I was stopped and detained. After 7 hours of fear and confusion, two officers from Mumbai arrived and flew me to Mumbai. 'We'd like you to come with us for some questions'.

At that point, nothing was clear. It seemed as if they were lost or misguided. It was a moment of confusion, to be honest. I was blank, but I followed them.

As soon as we reached the headquarters, five customs officers placed me in the interrogation room. I was sure it was some sort of a misunderstanding. However, I was nervous and scared; there was this bad feeling in the air, and I wasn't prepared for it.

The customs officers were Indians and didn't speak English at all, except one of them who managed to speak a little better for me to understand what they were asking, 'Mr Barry Hulse, three years ago we seized a package with your details on it since then, we've been looking for you'.

It clicked on me, and I realised what he was talking about.

The package goes back to 2006 when I travelled to Goa with my girlfriend. There, I met my friend E, who was on vacation with his girlfriend as well. This friend was someone I trusted and admired. He was struggling with drug addiction, and I was helping him through that as well; we were really close.

Our time in Goa was fantastic; all of us went partying and exchanged conversations. When the time to return back home was near, I decided we should go out and buy some gifts for our family. We went to the Anjuna Flea Market in Goa; Anjuna Flea Market is a vibrant market that is located quite near Anjuna Beach and is popular for souvenirs and unique materials at low prices.

The place was huge; you could wander and practically get lost in it for hours, full of antiques, deals, and potentially magical finds. The place would feel kaleidoscopic in the mere first few seconds. We wandered, and I bought a couple of T-shirts, Garnier products, decorative ornaments and knickknacks for my family.

Later, I calculated the luggage and realised it was more than the allowed load; the last time this happened, I remember I had to pay £150 extra for the over luggage. And I was certainly in no mood for that! Since everything else was of higher priority, I decided to let go of the gifts I bought. My friend, however, suggested I shouldn't just let them go to waste but rather have the gifts posted directly. I filled out the declaration form and handed photocopies of my passport and documents to my friend, as he said he'd go and post it. This person was someone I had known for years, so I didn't think anything could go wrong; it all seemed conventional at that time.

A month later, I still hadn't received the gifts; I tried to contact E numerous times to no avail. Besides, they were just gifts worth £50 anyway; it never bothered me enough.

I cleared my side of the story and asked them what the issue was really about because I was still confused. All I could think of was how is a package of gifts of any concern here or anywhere. What was going on here? What they said after sent shivers all over my body…..

'Mr Barry, £350 worth of Diazepam was found in that package with your details on it'.

'What'?

I was shocked. The horror was written all over my face. Maybe, that was the reason the officers didn't really suspect me, either. They could see I was completely unaware of this. While I could see the clouds clearing their way, I didn't know there was a second spell on its way, and this time, it had destruction on its mind.

'Mr Barry, I'll ask you again. Are you certain you had nothing to do with this'?

All I could say in a stammering manner was, 'Officer, I…I don't know how to tell you this, but I can never even imagine something like this'!

These people are trained to read between the lines, and they could see I was innocent. They made me sign a ten-page statement in which was my story of how I got stuck in this mess. It was all in Hindi, but the officer who spoke English helped me understand it.

However, when the officers were done, for now, they arranged a hotel for me and asked me to pay for two nights. They further instructed me to leave my luggage there. I assumed it was because they believed me;

they had to. I wasn't lying, and they could certainly tell from my body language. While all of this was happening, the customs officers were still investigating the case and caught their eye on the second address mentioned on the paperwork, which I was afraid to talk about as I was already frightened.

Twist in the tale; there were two packages that were to be posted. I had filled out two declaration forms, but looking at the amount of illegal possession present in just one, I was afraid of even discussing the other. I felt like it would make things more complicated. Being disorientated due to lack of sleep and agitated with all that was happening around me, or I simply wasn't thinking straight. I told them that my friend had misplaced the first paperwork, so he came back with a second form. I chose not to reveal the second box when they initially asked me.

Besides, they were just asking about the first package anyway. They didn't have the boxes with them at that moment; the boxes had been at a go-down in Mumbai since 2006 when they were seized. It turned out that the second box had a similar amount of Diazepam in it.

That's when the whole situation escalated. The customs officers came barging in and shouted in Hindi; they were speaking words that were completely foreign to me, but I understood what they meant. I assumed they were saying, 'You lied to us! You manipulated us'!

Before I could add anything to my defence, the third officer, who thankfully spoke English, interrupted with, 'You tried tricking us with your "I am innocent" game'!

They assumed I lied and tried to hide the second package while trying my best to manipulate them as well. They had already made up their minds, so anything I said further was of no use. The customs officers soon involved the Mumbai Police. One official of the Mumbai Police came to me and said something in Hindi that I could barely understand. But the context was certainly something like, 'So, you thought you could fool us'?

Their expressions and tone of voice helped me through the communication barrier. I could tell he was extremely aggravated. Clearly, after finding out about the second box, they had turned against me. Their attitude had completely changed, and they started to get a bit violent. Out of nowhere, there came a sudden hit to my face, and they continued. They battered me up in an attempt to get a confession. I was quite shaken up by the beatings. For me, it was abuse as I was completely innocent.

After this, the real struggle began…

'Once all struggle is grasped, miracles are possible'.

—Mao Zedong

Chapter Two

Ironic how we grow up thinking we're finally old enough to face the world on our own while we need the ones we love the most in times of dire need.

I thought I was an independent person living the life I created myself until it all hit me; we are never truly independent. There will always come a time when you realise how important relationships are and how dependent you are upon them. A tree might have strong roots but still blossoms better with others planted aside from it. In like manner, we, as humans, need support, whether emotional or physical. But surviving alone is a struggle only the bravest can behold.

When I was finally allowed to make one call, I decided to call my girlfriend. I didn't want to bother my mother unless it was necessary. I explained to my girlfriend the whole scenario, to which she panicked but chose to remain calm. I also told her not to tell anyone at this point. I thought the worse that could crop up would be a payable fine or getting bailed out indefinitely. I mean, at that moment, I did not look at my situation as an *imprisonable* offence.

She told me not to worry as she tried to figure things out and provided me with contacts of the best NDPS Lawyers in Mumbai (Narcotics Drugs and Psychotropic Substances) and soon connected me to a lawyer named Taraq Sayed. Taraq Sayed was a very famous lawyer in Mazgaon, Mumbai. His speciality was NDPS (Narcotic Drugs and Psychotropic Substances) and NCB (Narcotic Control Bureau). Unfortunately, I was in a country where laws were quite different from what they were back home. For instance, I was told I could not have a lawyer until my statement was made. Whereas in England, your lawyer must be present when you are giving a statement.

The sun is also a star. It burns itself to give us light, while all we do is blame it for its heat. To see the good in people is an art. The good is never transparent; it is always hidden behind the clouds of something that seems the opposite. The good, however, is always there.

It was as if the whole state was coming to get me. Every gateway of escape seemed to be locked. However, amidst this misery came a moment of relief when I had a chat with Taraq Sayed; he seemed to have a good command of English. Just to know there was someone around who could understand me was a reassurance. He said to me over the phone, 'Don't worry! I will meet you in court then. Just be calm and do not stress'!

Honestly, that quite helped. I mean, it did not completely unburden me, but I admit, it was a moment of relief. I felt a bit lightweight and happier.

Anyway, it was around 5:30 in the morning, so I got some rest. We were still in the office, so I slept on a small bench there. It had been so long, and I was probably experiencing jet lag as well. It wasn't a sound sleep as the bench wasn't comfortable, and well, the whole situation was awful. I noticed they locked me up while I was asleep.

However, the next day, it was 10:30 in the morning, and they told me to go get washed, so I brushed my teeth and wiped that sleepy face of mine. They took me to some market to get my photographs done on my way to court.

Upon arriving at the downtown market, the sight I saw was horrible. People were staring at me and judging me as if they had never seen a white person before. They were even pointing fingers. I cannot forget all those stares. The officers did not handcuff me, but they were continuously holding my wrists. Their expressions were as if they were proud of catching a white person. It was a situation where they were the fishermen, and I was the big fish, and they were showing me off to the market. It was horrible, I'll tell you. I felt like an alien, as if I had already lost the battle I was fighting. It was like many against one.

'Pain and humiliation is always amusing when it happens to someone else'.

—Eileen Cook, The Hanging Girl

After the photographs were done, we then arrived at the court. The officers got engaged in some paperwork for the judge. The pressure was too much until I heard someone thirty steps ahead of me saying, 'Don't worry, I'll get you out'.

He was in a lawyer's suit, and I remember when I had a chat with Taraq Sayed, he said he'd come to meet me at court. I assumed the person offering me help would be him. He had to be.

He said, 'How much money do you have on you'?

Well, I had obviously brought pounds with me, but I spent 2,000 rupees on the hotel for two nights, as the officers asked me to. So, I was left with 5,500 rupees which I handed over to Taraq Sayed.

In a world of deceit, corruption and evil, innocence is a curse.

As if the worst hadn't already happened to me, I was sitting there on the bench observing the surroundings. People were sitting on the floors or waiting when a tall man in a suit came to me and said, 'Barry Hulse'?

I said, 'Yes'?

'It's nice to meet you. I am Taraq Sayed'.

'Wait...what? No. He's Taraq Sayed', I said while pointing at the person who was supposed to be right beside me.

'Uh, no! I am Taraq Sayed', said the tall man in the suit. This went on in a loop at least three to four times. He told me about the chat we had, and I couldn't explain how muddled I was.

What was going on here?

Where am I?

Who are these people?

These were the exact questions running through my mind. I told him what had happened and how I had ended up giving my money to an imposter.

It turned out the man wasn't Taraq Sayed and that I had lost the money I had to someone who was a cheater. However, the real Taraq Sayed told me about the corruption that was deeply embedded in the system and almost everywhere in this state. He was equally frustrated as me. He assured me he'd get my money back, though. He said the person was just a lawyer like him but, obviously, the lowest of the low.

So, then, my case came up in front of the judge. I couldn't understand a word because everything was in Hindi. I stayed silent and observed. All I got at the end of the conversation was that the next hearing would be after two weeks.

When we came out of the court, Taraq Sayed came to me and said, 'So, here's the thing, you will have to go to prison'.

He sighed.

'What? What did you say'? I abruptly replied, thinking I possibly misunderstood.

'Yes, mate. You will have to go to prison', he repeated.

'But…why? I haven't done anything'?! I tried to protest.

'Barry, it is just procedure, and everything will turn out fine', he said, reassuring me although it didn't seem convincing.

I remember I kept asking him anxiously, 'For how long? But for how long'?

I didn't even give him a chance to answer the question. He took a pause and stared at me. He put both his hands on my shoulders to calm me down. When I finally paused, he said, 'For sixty days'.

I remember my response and the exact burst of emotions I felt.

'SIXTY DAYS'???

It was as if my voice was somehow held back, and I was shouting while panicking in a low voice.

'Sixty days'? It was just that I couldn't believe I was at a point in time where I was being told I would have to spend sixty days of my life in jail!

Taraq Sayed added to calm me down, 'The investigation takes sixty days'.

What is with this world anyway? Why does it give if it has to take it back? Why does it pull you up if it has to drop you down again? Isn't it better not to have felt happier than to realise the intensity of it not being there anymore? The world works in mysterious ways. And, at that moment, I looked up with tears in my eyes, wondering what would become of me.

Unable to shake the conviction that the day was hanging over me like a guillotine. I was certain that this was the exact moment, the very second where my life would be cleaved in two, a before and an, after all, what was good and interesting about me, that made me a person worthy of attention would be stripped away, and whatever remained would be thrust, unrecognizable, into the void that awaited. Nevertheless, I continued with whatever was coming towards me. There wasn't any choice anyway.

We went a bit further outside the court to eat something. In front of me was the imposter who took money from me. I couldn't believe my eyes. He was munching with his people with MY MONEY! The real Taraq Sayed said it was nothing to worry about. He approached the imposter in hopes of getting back my money. Well, he did, but just 1,500 rupees, of course, what was left of it. Taraq Sayed said this would come in handy for my days in prison.

Taraq Sayed left, and it was just the five customs officers and me. It was 7:30 in the evening; they took me to Arthur Road, a jail there in Mumbai……

On my way there, I had thoughts rushing through my mind. Even though Taraq Sayed gave me hope, he was also not afraid to call a spade a spade; he told me that the next sixty days were going to be tough and I would need to be strong. I was never prepared to spend even six days of my life in jail. I was anxious, scared, and I was depressed. These sixty days would be the darkest days of my life, one of the many frightful thoughts I had that day, that moment. Deep down, I knew it was absurd. However, knowing this did not keep me from anxiously glancing outside as if everyone around me were holding actual blades at me.

I was desperate; I was craving a hug from my loved ones. I just wanted to go back. I wondered what will my son do and think for these sixty days. My son was eighteen; how would I explain everything that happened? Would he even believe me? And my mum? The torment she'll go through for sixty days?

Mothers have that magic; they know everything, every detail. Even the pain that fails to transmit from the heart to the brain. They worry about the tiniest things, things that do not even bother us. I remember, what felt like ages now, how my mother's face brought calm and serenity to an exhausting day. Her eyes shining like bright lights would cast a mesmerising golden hue on everything. It was the sort of light that, even in the most hell-bent situation, you'd want to look into with renewed awe.

Still, in my own thoughts, I realised the van had stopped. We had reached my grim fate, the beginning of my nightmare. Right in front of me was my lot in life that was forcefully brought upon me.

I stepped out of the van and was told to step towards the gate in front of me. The very gate I had never imagined walking towards. While walking, I thought to myself, *I'll have to live sixty days of my life as a criminal.*

Even though I was completely innocent, I had never ever done anything remotely illegal, let alone criminal. Despite that, I had this embarrassment and shame inside of me. I kept thinking of my family, my son. I didn't deserve this, and neither did they. He wasn't supposed to even go through thoughts of his dad being in jail. Though I wasn't even sure if the news broke to him this early, whenever it did, I just hoped it doesn't affect him.

Currently, my mind felt split, as though there were two voices in my head, and I was swinging from one to the other. The rational voice kept pointing out that it was deplorable to cower before life circumstances. *Why me?* said the other voice. Sure, I was strong-willed, but the other voice was acting like a stubborn child wanting to know why they were being punished. But this so-called luck was all I had to blame for now.

Children are quite fragile, you know. They are the most delicate of beings. The tiniest inconvenience can break their hearts and shatter the ground they walk on.

Finally, I was standing right in front of the gate of Arthur Road. The gate was huge with a grey-bricked wall. I could tell it was quite old as the paint was coming off as well. Besides, the Arthur Jail was the oldest and largest prison which was built in 1926 by the British. It was later upgraded into the central prison of Mumbai. I gasped for breath as the guards were instructed to open it. I was having a mini panic attack, if that's even a thing. My blood pressure was increasing, I had cold sweats, and I felt shortness of breath. Sixty days might not be a huge timespan for many, but for me, it was more than I could take in, mostly because I did not even do anything to deserve this.

'Fear is the mind-killer'.

—Frank Herbert, Dune

We went through the metal gate, which was rusted, into this doorway. It opened to a circle-shaped open area. The hall was completely empty, not a sign of life. I remember looking everywhere, just blank. On the left was a small desk, and on the right were a couple of offices which were probably of the senior superintendents. They sat me down and left me alone for like two hours. The hall was the place where all the prisoners usually congregated to be escorted to court. I was so tired, and I hadn't slept for days as it was a night of celebration the day before it all went down. I was disoriented by that time, so I slept on the rock-like floor in the hall for two hours. I was told I would have a court meeting every two weeks. I was hopeful.

'*Hope'* What is hope? A belief that there is something better on the other side of this darkness, on the other side of our sword. Give a person a chance to believe that something better lies just around the corner, in reach but out of sight, and they will give everything they have to get a glimpse of that future. Sometimes, that belief is all you have left. All that keeps you going. *Bring on the blades,* I thought. I was so tired of my own mind it would be a relief.

'They say a person needs just three things to be truly happy in this world: someone to love, something to do, and something to hope for'.

—Tom Bodett

After I woke up, a guard came to me and asked me if I had money on me. I thought to myself, *What if he was like the person who took my 5500 rupees?*

I said, 'No, I do not have any money on me'.

Although I did, I had that 1500 rupees, which Taraq Sayed got back from the fraud; I had hidden it under my undergarments. By now, I had realised that I'd come across people who would try to get money out of any situation, especially since I was a Western foreigner. It is generally perceived in developing societies that people living in the West are always loaded with lots of money, and this very concept was going to leave me without any money.

The guard was persistent; maybe it was because somebody told him I had money. He kept asking me if I had the money four to five times.

However, it wasn't like that. He explained to me that I could open a prisoner account where money could be transferred from the outside; as in, my loved ones could send me money. It'll help me buy essentials like soap, toothpaste and cigarettes etc., and the amount spent would automatically be deducted from the account. Basically, the prisoners weren't allowed to have cash on them physically, and it was quite understandable. The account was called the PPC account, and I figured I would need the daily essentials to get through the next 60 days.

This was not even a percent of what Arthur Road actually was like. After we were done with the paperwork for the account, I was taken to the other building of the Jail. It was like a small building which I found out was previously used as a place of worship for the Muslims, Hindus,

Christians and all the religious sects on certain festivals. This place was an open area as well. There were like sixty people over here.

I remember just standing there staring at all the buildings. The place was huge; to be precise, I was standing in front of long concrete buildings with metal gates to enter and exit. The buildings were known as the Barracks. There was the Anda Barrack, which was a high-security area. Then there was the After Barrack, where the prisoners were held if they came in from the court after 5:30 PM. Basically, in Maharashtra, the states of Mumbai and Goa are in, has the same prison timings. Every prison is locked by 5:30 PM, so if you come back late, you'll be held in the After Barrack till the next day.

It was as if I had this filming camera fixed in my eyes. I even zoomed in to notice the details. This prison I was in was a whole different world. I could see the paint falling off the buildings, cracks in drywall, especially over doors and windows, there were water spots on the ceiling and stains from plumbing leaks and window leaks. What was worse was that I wasn't even inside my cell till then. This was just the outside of the building; I was panicking about what was waiting for me inside.

I just looked above at the number of floors present in each building. I wondered how many people would have been present there. The place, I repeat, was huge! I had several questions popping up at that time. Questions like, *What will this jail be like? Will I have to fight in there for my place? Will there be violence? Will I come across sexual predators?*

There were a lot of fearful questions, I tell you. But the one that worried me the most was, will they accept me because I was a foreigner. Am I even going to understand anybody? What if no one understands me?

It was 9:00 PM in the evening, and the Sunday was towards its end, so they took me to the After Barrack. The After Barrack was at the bottom, so the way to it was daunting.

What I saw afterwards was a sight of horror. I mean, I was shocked to the core. I remember just looking around the place and feeling paralysed for a moment. The After Barrack is usually empty, but sometimes there can be just four people and sometimes more. When I came in, there were a total of fifteen lads. These fifteen people were the ones who were arrested the same day.

It was a stone area with chunks of concrete missing from the walls. There was no paint. On the side, there was a little washing area where you could wash the dishes or things like that. There were no beds, just the cemented floor. The lights were only on the ceilings, along with the ceiling fans, which were placed every fifteen meters. The lights were almost of no use as the roof was at an enormous height. The place reminded me of my mum's cellar. To be precise, it was dark, damp, cold and dirty.

It was utter distress; I asked myself where the beds were. How are people surviving this mess? However, there was this one person who could speak good English, so it filled the communication gap. He was from Nigeria.

In the middle of our conversation, a man came in and said it was time for food. He made us sit in two lines, seven people on each side. The man who instructed us has been a prisoner here for a long time, so he was appointed as the warder in charge of that place as there weren't any other guards.

So, the warder pulled out a metal container with a handle. It must have been two feet high. The container had *daal* in it; I'd say the *daal* over there is like the lentils we have, along with some green vegetables. We were all handed tin plates and a small tin bowl. After serving us the *daal*, they passed the *roti* down. *Roti* was like a seven-inch flat bread which wasn't of very good quality. It was dry and tasteless.

Speaking of which, the *daal* they served was equally disgusting. We were also served rice. I had no spoon, and people had no soap to wash their hands, so I just couldn't eat. I had maybe two bites of it, and I was done.

I kept looking around at people in mere shock. I thought to myself, *How could someone be okay with this?* These people were literally enjoying their meal.

Above all, they were comfortable with the way they were told to sit. I couldn't even fold my legs.

Amongst all this anxiety, it was a relief to speak to someone who understood and was in the same situation, though the Nigerian was in for violating immigration or visa laws. But I could relate in a way that he was an outsider and didn't seem to like the place much either.

When the clock hit 10:30 PM, the warder came in again and said it was time for us to sleep. I thought to myself, *Sleep? Here?*

He gave us no pillow, no sheet, just a mat which was similar to a yoga mat and a 4 ft. wide *kumbul.*

So, I lay down on the cemented floor on that yoga mat. How could I sleep there? My eyes were wide open. I couldn't sleep in a place like this. I could hear the voices of people whispering; it was echoing everywhere. It was as if the walls were talking. And there were small barred-rusted windows from where I could hear men shouting, fighting, and even laughing. It was uncanny. The dim light, the air whispering itself in your ears and the sudden haunting sounds, it was impossible for me to sleep in a place like this.

While these thoughts invaded my mind, I saw a small shadow right in front of me. The shadow had two bright eyes, and it was approaching me. I was an inch away from a mental breakdown when I realised it was a cat with four kittens. I don't hate cats, but I just can't have them near me. So, I got up and tried to shoo them away. When it was finally over, the next thing I see are these big black ants marching everywhere.

I said to myself in despair, *Oh God! Where am I?* It made me twitchy, of course. I wasn't used to this. I was already starting to feel sick of it; this was just night one.

I was restless and nervous; I couldn't sleep. I was flustered; my only thought that night was that I had to serve fifty-nine more days in the same place, with the same people, eat the same food and sleep on the same cold surface full of black ants.

It was maybe one or two in the morning; I was lying down with heavy eyes, the background slowly blurring out with a deep voice in my head

'One day down, Barry, fifty-nine more to go'.

'People don't always get what they deserve in this world'.

— Lemony Snicket

Chapter Three

You may carry the strength of a lion, but there will come a time when trauma will have you tremble like a sheep. At that moment, the best thing to do is remember...remember that you have the strength of a lion.

It doesn't matter how red-blooded you are; the moment you hurt yourself, you will bleed. Trauma does that to you; it moves you to an extent you truly begin to understand what it feels to 'live the pain'. The minute you two connect, it follows you everywhere. But maybe that is what we all need once in our lives, an incident that breaks the pattern, an episode of fear, pain and torment. Sometimes, we've got to break into pieces to get back together.

I told myself that this was just a phase, a juncture that shall pass by. The constant reminder that my situation was temporarily kept my sanity intact. It was 6:30 in the morning when they woke us up. While everyone was struggling to get up, I, despite not having a good sleep, woke up eagerly to see the light of the day. I just sat there, desperate to get out of that dungeon, but there wasn't a single movement from the guards.

Approximately 20 minutes later, they opened the gates. For me, it was the gates to a different dimension, as if they allowed me to have a peek at heaven, to enjoy the feel of it. I clearly, couldn't stand this place. While the gates were opening, people who were still lying around got up immediately and approached the gate. I stepped towards the gate; I remember before stepping outside, I took a deep breath to prepare myself for what I was about to encounter. I no longer had expectations, I knew I had to bear this for some time, so I accepted it. It was a kind of walkway around the barrack; people marched outside towards the bathing area. What they called the bathing area was something anomalously new to me. It was somewhat of a brick structure, with two gullies a foot deep and a pipe sticking out of each end. People were filling up buckets with water to bathe.

While I was noticing people and their actions, the breakfast came in. It was in metal containers. Upon this sight, people formed queues holding their respective plates and pots. It looked more like school premises at that moment than a prison. Which was good; I mean, anything is better than a prison, I suppose. These short-lived positive thoughts, in a nutshell, ensured that I could have a rather bearable time at the prison. I don't really know about others who were unfortunate enough to end up in prison, but it really does feel miserable. And if your mind is shut down to a point where you cannot even process such thoughts, then it probably means it will be tougher than anything else.

I picked up my breakfast and sat down to feed my stomach. I started to recall all the times when I was rushing out in the morning, and my mother would call me back, insisting I gulp down a few sips of tea and some toast. It always felt ordinary. But while I was in prison, it came off as a memory I couldn't put away.

While I had my breakfast, I was called into the superintendent's office. Even though everyone had already finished their meal, I was dragging it as I didn't quite like it; yellow rice for breakfast was not so appealing. I quickly wrapped it up, sipped the tea and went towards the office. It was around ten then, when I entered the office; I saw a woman there from the British Embassy, which is based in Mumbai. The moment I saw her, I breathed a sigh of relief. It was as if she had lifted a burden off my shoulders. What I had in mind was this person in front of me was someone who enjoyed a great deal of high power. This person is from the British Embassy. My angel of mercy is here; maybe I am getting out early.

'Mr Barry? Uh, Mr Barry'?

'Huh? Oh yes. Yes'! I replied to the lady the moment I came back to reality.

We talked about the whole situation, and what she told me disappointed me a little, but I guess by now, I had seen enough to know anything was possible. Even in a situation where we do not see anything bad coming our way, it does. Life is a rollercoaster where it can throw hurdles your way as if someone had 'notified' you in advance. Alas! That's not how it goes.

'Mr Barry, I apologise as the British Embassy cannot involve itself in this matter, but we sure are willing to help. We will provide you with a list of lawyers that might speed up your case'.

I was not given a specific reason as to why they did not involve themselves in my situation, but I had a clue. It was definitely due to diplomatic reasons.

Anyway, she gave me a small bar of soap, toothpaste, and a brush. It was clear that she was staying in a hotel, and she brought it from there. However, I was grateful for any help in my current desperate situation. She told me she had a chat with my family and that all of them knew where I was and that I was doing just fine.

As soon as she told me that they were okay as well and were praying for my safe return, I broke down. I mean, I wasn't upset; I was relieved to hear something from my family. I got so emotional. I had been acting all tough and unaffected in prison; this was bound to happen. One more reason for my breakdown was that I finally got to meet someone who completely understood me and was from my homeland. I had been desperate to meet someone who spoke my language fluently and was from British culture. So, it was an emotional outburst, which was very much needed to keep me going.

'Sometimes, breaking down is the bravest thing you can do'.

—Vironika Tugaleva

She gave me a list of some of the most reputable NDPS lawyers, but I refused as I was already engaged with Taraq Sayed and quite honestly, I was satisfied with him. I wasn't in the frame of mind to start over and place my trust in someone new. I told her that I was okay with the lawyer I had right now.

After the meeting, I was called in to form a queue with everyone else from the After Barrack. The situation was confusing, but thankfully I had that Nigerian friend now. Everything seemed less of a mess. Having a companion means a great deal at times. Have a look at your friends; we do take them for granted. It is at times like these that you begin to realise that having even one person to talk to is a blessing.

The embassy official gave me books on how to survive in this prison, which I guess was a rule to distribute books to every new British prisoner. The books were based on self-help, yoga and on how to stay safe and healthy. Everyone was appointed a separate barrack according to their offences.

For instance, the number eleven barrack was known as the Murder Barrack, so people who had committed homicides were sent to the number eleven barrack. Since my new friend was in for immigration violation, he was allotted the 6 no. barrack, and I was allotted the 8 no. This made me a little anxious as I did not know anyone else but him. I thought to myself if there was any way to allot us the same barracks, but obviously, there wasn't. The 8 no. barrack, which was the NDPS barrack, was allotted to every drug addict or smuggler. For me, this was a place I could never fit in. I kept reminding myself I was innocent. For me, every person in there was someone I could never relate to. However, I did as I was told; I stepped towards the 8 no. barrack.

I walked in, and what I saw was an utter nightmare. I had never seen something so gut-churning and revolting as the sight I saw the moment I set foot in there. It was almost like a slum; plastic bags and everyone's belongings were hung on the wall, and washing lines filled the place with prisoners' wet clothes. Each barrack had a two-floor structure, and each floor had over 200 prisoners, although the capacity was 80. Even though the place was bigger than the After Barrack, it was still congested as people were lying on the floor in groups, and their belongings were dispersed. I had to be careful while walking to avoid stepping on something or someone.

While I was in the middle of a comprehensive examination of the place I was allotted, I witnessed something horrific. A person there was having a fit; I saw foam coming out of his mouth. It was a very disturbing sight to see. But people there were dealing with the situation as if it was something usual. It turns out that since almost everyone here was a drug addict, the body needed heroin. And because it doesn't get the dose anymore, fits are a result of their absence. I looked at the man and thought to myself, *Why would anyone do that to themselves? Why would one punish himself like that? What was so alluring about these drugs anyway? It clearly destroys the personality and the life you create. Isn't that what we all think of drug addicts normally?*

Well, that was me. Behaving just as any other person would.

Moving on, an Indian man walked towards me and said in a low tone, 'Don't stay in this barrack. Come on upstairs'!

This guy, despite being an Indian, was western-educated. He said he would take me to the upper floor, and I could join the *Handi* group. The *Handi* group was just a group of between 3 to approximately 12 prisoners who would eat together. It sounded like a good idea. I followed him upstairs and was introduced to the people there. The *Handi* group consisted of a guy from France, a guy from the Philippines, and then there was this Indian guy who approached me. I was warmly welcomed. Everyone from that group was somehow similar to me. I felt relieved and comfortable.

Although it was the same situation there, I could see bugs and insects everywhere. I felt welcomed in the group because everyone there was almost a foreigner, so it was like a mixed foreigner group. The place was huge, but because of the sheer number of prisoners and overcrowding, every chore was carried out in the same place, even the washing, eating and sleeping.

The good thing about the *Handi* group was that they provided you with the masala and other flavours to add to the food for further taste. Everyone there who received a money order would provide these, and Rey, a Philippine, would do the chores, like setting everything out and washing dishes afterwards etc. However, the place wasn't all comforting. I still saw cases of fright every now and then, and even though it used to shake me up, I used to look at everyone and think I was somehow in a better situation than all of them. My situation isn't as bad as theirs is.

'You can do this, Barry, you can do this', I sighed. It felt like there was a boulder on my chest, my lungs felt tight, but I had to breathe. I kept repeating these words as if I wanted my brain to memorise them and act upon them.

The very first night, I was introduced to a lot of different people; again, it was shocking as some of them had been stuck here for four years or more, just waiting for their trial to finish. Mostly, they would ask about my case, and I'd explain its Diazepam tablets, to which they'd say, 'No tension, or don't take tension because you'll definitely get off'.

I remember this one person who was there for two years on the grounds of marijuana; many people were going through a lot more than they actually deserved. However, these cases that I was introduced to every now and then really frightened me, but I kept telling myself this was not how it was going to turn out for me. There is no way I will end up as bad as these other people; I am a British citizen, after all.

Every day it was the same ritual; the breakfast came in at 7:00 am in the morning. It was quiet from the court and the officials for days, but I was satisfied as I knew the investigation was in process. They didn't approach me as I had given my statement. What more could they possibly get out of me!?

So, at that point, there were no further questions. The rules here were quite stressful. The bedding was a 2 x 6 feet rag, not much thicker than a bed sheet. When the warder used to whistle, everyone was supposed to run and grab the best possible place he could get. Since I was a bit hesitant about this culture, my group managed to get me a place to sleep.

That morning, when they opened the gates, my friends took me to the toilet and handed over a large jug to me. I was new here, and the showering and bathroom system and the procedure were a shock to me. These people made me realise this isn't the Western culture. The place was situated behind the barrack, which was usually used for bathing. It was shallow, sort of one foot to the ground, where the water was running.

While I was struggling to accept the bathroom ways, I saw that people don't even bother washing it away. That is what almost made me puke. The doors to the bathroom were so low that every now and then, people were coming and peeking in to see if there was an empty bathroom somewhere. Besides, the doors of the toilets could barely be locked, I literally didn't go to the toilet for two days, but I knew I couldn't run from this forever. In short, the place wasn't very private. I was desperate for a private space. I just wanted to breathe alone for once.

But it was so crowded; this was definitely not possible. It was a very confined place, plus the *gentry* was not something I could place myself in. But since I was a new face and not everyone was familiar with me, people kept coming up to me and asking my name and story. I remember it made me paranoid. I was coming to a point where people thought of me as aggressive and aggravated. I was sick and tired of hearing '*No Tension*', '*No Tension*', from everybody. I just needed a moment for myself, but I wasn't getting one. During those days, I saw a lot of people suffering from seizures, as their bodies needed the drug.

This was basically my routine for the week. Using the toilet for me was a great deal of a struggle. Squatting to do my business in a hole in the ground and then washing instead of using toilet paper was a whole new experience for me. Obviously, showering there would have been a greater deal of struggle. Finally, there came a day when showering became necessary, and I could not run from it anymore. My friends introduced me to how to shower, basically.

You had to have buckets to shower, so my friends gave me an old one. People there were very possessive about their buckets. There were fights every day for it, and if someone couldn't get the bucket, they would use their metal pots as substitutes which were for their food. I thought to myself, *These metal pots are only 4 inches deep. How do these people even manage?*

Anyway, after you have got the bucket, you then align. The water flows from the pipeline, so you have to fill the bucket with water from the pipeline. There were two pipes at the end of each gully area; one had a minimum of eight people around it. These prisoners were pushing their metal pots under the pipe for a cup full of water, and arguments and fights were usual every morning. The other pipe was for the prisoners who had a bucket. This meant if you were around tenth in the queue, you knew that in 30-40 minutes, you would get a full bucket of water.

Among other daily chores, the wardens and prison guards used to enter every morning and do a headcount before opening the gates. This was to ensure all the prisoners were present and there had not been any inconveniences. And if any of the prisoners were found sleeping, they would just whack their sticks on them to wake them up.

At night, you were provided with a two feet space for your bedding; the people who had been there a little bit longer had a fixed place against the wall, and the new ones were forced to get what was left of the remaining space in the centre.

When the warden used to blow the whistle, people used to rush towards their named places and roll their beddings out. Since I had people in my group who already had their places here, I got a proper place to sleep for that night.

For the next week, this was my daily routine. I woke up every day to the same people, the same food, the same horrific stories and strange encounters.

I remember people coming up to me and touching my tattoos. My initial reactions were as if I was ready for a fight, but they explained they just wanted to feel how it was. I clearly remember a person coming up to me and asking if this was some sort of paint, as he was unaware of what tattoos were.

I explained to them that the process is quite complex and requires a needle and also that it is permanent. They were clearly struck in awe. They obviously had never seen anything like this before.

My life for a week was a never-ending void. I was starting to feel numb; it was almost as if the light inside me was starting to dim a little. But the most pressing question of all was: 'How am I going to spend the rest of the days here'. Honestly, I had started to give up on all the energy I had. The nights were shattered, and the stars shivered. And as I tried to look around to find the solitude, I realised I still had 53 days to go.

They tell you to never give up on your hopes; they advise you to hold on to hope forever. But what they never tell you is that forever is deception. And sometimes, God does fail you!

Chapter Four

They say time heals everything; what if time is your wound? What if the only thing that hurts is the time that passes by? The clock ticking is like a needle pricking, and with every second, it pierces deeper into your skin.

If I had been given a pen and paper and told to write down the worst I could expect from my fate, I still wouldn't have come to this. We are hit by situations that we would have considered unreal from afar. All of a sudden, within seconds, you can be shifted into a different dimension.

It wasn't easy to accept what was happening, really. Every day, I had thoughts of escaping, but the courage and planning to actually do so were nil. I saw people every day paying the guards some extra cash so that they stop being a prick towards them, especially when they were out for their court meetings. The guards, if paid, let them relax and move around for a while. I remember I counted every single day. I remember staring at the wall in the middle of the night and reminding myself, *Only fifty-six days left, Barry. Only forty-nine days left, Barry....*

When you don't like the moment you're in, it feels a bit longer. Imagine spending sixty days, which felt more like sixty years to me.

However, I had court appearances between these sixty days. Every 14 days, I had to appear in court. I was always ready for it, but when the time came near, I used to lose hope. I kept telling myself I could not do this anymore.

After three weeks of being in that jail, I finally got a court date. Thankfully, I had brought a t-shirt and jeans with me. I wore them to the court that day. The guard came and squashed fifteen guards and twenty prisoners at the back of the van. It was so congested I started to panic. This was probably the first time I thought to myself I was fine in prison.

However, Taraq Sayed told me not to worry because this was just a mandatory procedure until my charge sheet was produced. A charge sheet is basically the sheet with every bit of the evidence they have against you. He told me it takes sixty days to produce a charge sheet. One benefit I had through a court meeting was that I got to have a chat with my family. I had mixed feelings while talking to my mother.

I mean, I was extremely happy and relieved to hear her voice, but at the same time, I was emotionally drained and depressed because I missed her more. My mother was crying and kept telling me how concerned she was for my safety. She was also concerned about the little details like how I must be sleeping, what I must be eating and how are the people here treating me.

A mother's love can never be compared. She was concerned for the exact same things that troubled me there. I cannot even begin to explain how much I miss her; if there was a way for me to just escape, I would have at that moment. I was desperate to hug her. I kept telling her, while hiding the pain in my voice, that this was something temporary and it wasn't as bad as it sounded. I remember she was crying, and I said, 'Mum, everything is okay'.

She started crying even more. I couldn't understand why she did that at the moment, but now I know. She knew I was lying, that nothing was okay. The problem is that I had never been away for more than two weeks, and this was three weeks straight. My family, especially my mother, wasn't used to it.

My son wasn't used to it either, though. They were traumatised by the situation.

I reassured mum everything was okay and told them it was just sixty days; I'll do it. While I was reassuring her, I remember physically feeling a heavy weight in my chest. It was like I was lying to her, deceiving her.

My mum and I have been like friends, so there has never been a situation where I chose to lie to her. I was emotionally destroyed at that moment.

I just wanted to turn back to the child who comes home, runs and hugs his mother and tells her everything he feels. But I couldn't. I knew my mother. It would have worried her sick. And I needed her to be alright; I don't think I had the energy to survive any other trauma at that moment. These thoughts that were continuously running in my head made me freeze for a min. I had this heavy feeling in my chest, and I was speechless. Even though I had so many answers, questions and things to express, I was speechless.

I had really scary thoughts invading my mind while talking to her. I was on the verge of breaking down because I had this question bothering me at the back of my head. I wondered if I would ever be able to hear her voice again. I was worried if I would ever be able to see her face again. A mother's love is undying. And I needed that undying love; I needed hope. I wanted someone to run to as soon as I got out of there.

I ended the call, took a deep breath and wiped my tears. I reminded myself I am lucky because I have someone who loves me unconditionally. However, then, we headed back to the prison and back to my barrack. I was so low; there were still forty days left. I desperately needed motivation. I kept reminding myself that no matter how bad it was, time would pass.

I did survive three weeks here, so I can survive forty days as well. I told myself I was almost halfway there; sometimes, it was a motivational sentence, and sometimes, it was the most demotivating truth of my life.

A few days later, I realised the Christmas period was around the corner. The good thing about this place was that even though everyone was different from the other person, one thing united us all, and that was the fact that we were all prisoners.

There were two Indians here that helped us, me in particular, wash clothes. My routine was strict there; at exactly 11:30, I went to grab newspapers. There were newspapers which were Indian, and then there were newspapers which were in English. The English newspapers were *Indian Express*, *Times of India* and two or three others. While I used to manage my time by eating lunch and reading the newspaper, the gates used to open at exactly 3 o'clock in the afternoon. That is when everyone used to put down whatever they were doing and rush towards the gates. It was almost as if I was living the life of a robot. Every day we were doing the exact same thing and living the exact same life. There was never anything new in the routine.

My time in prison taught me something I would have never learned otherwise. There are two types of prisoners ones are the people who are convicted and sentenced to prison, while others are the ones who are prisoners of their minds. I, at that moment, was living as both. I saw people who were free, people who wouldn't even want to leave the prison. They were happy inside these dungeons. There was a point in time when I looked at these people and wondered if they were right. What if life outside is really not worth It? I mean, look at what it did to me. What if living like a robot was far better than living the life of a human?

Isn't it ironic how having free will sometimes becomes agonizing? Knowing you have a right, a power inside of you, but being caged instead?

Since Christmas was just around the corner, I was feeling empty. I never imagined I would have to celebrate such an occasion in prison. Grief is such a deep word. You can grieve over situations and events as well. You can grieve for people who are alive as well.

We usually associate grief with people who have passed away. We need to know that there are people in this world who grieve themselves. You grieve for the one you used to be. Some people die early; all there's left of them is a robotic, lifeless body, a body with no free will, waiting relentlessly to be buried.

Maybe hope is nothing but an empty promise. Or, maybe it is a deception people created for the ones who discovered the reality.

I saw people who were in there for years, people who were forgotten and people who were left in there for good. But what amazed me was their undying hope for someone to reach out to them. They strongly believed that someone would be waiting for them outside. I felt lucky sometimes. Because I kept receiving letters and cards from not just my family but from people I did not even know. It turns out people came to know about my situation and were supporting me in every way they could. I remember receiving wishes, cards and heartfelt letters.

I didn't feel like I was alone. I knew in my heart that there were people out there who loved me and were waiting for me. But living there forced me to go through negative thoughts. There were days when I had thoughts like maybe you're remembered because it's just been weeks.

The afternoons I spent there were quite boring, as all we did was walk, play chess and watch Indian soap operas, which I could barely understand. I found it funny, though; these Indian soap operas were quite emotional and unrealistic. There wasn't any productive thing to do, actually.

When Christmas arrived, I started receiving parcels, gifts, cards and even letters to give me hope. My friends, my family and even a lot of supporters wrote me things like '*Don't give up*' or '*You're not alone*'. I also received a diary and would jot down day-to-day things. I remember re-reading all of them from time to time. Receiving and replying back is a complex process; the packages and even letters are scrutinised by the officials and then passed over.

These efforts really did give me hope. I told myself I had to keep it together, if not for myself, then for all of these people. I cannot let them down when they are desperately waiting for me outside. This was the only thought giving me strength; the rest of it was just draining me instead. Those days are when I actually realised what depression is and how dangerous it can be. I found myself fighting my own thoughts. Trying to eliminate negativity, but it was as if the force was more powerful than me.

I remember this one person who was getting bailed out; instead of just picking up his stuff and rushing towards his freedom, he actually cried and begged to stay. I thought to myself, *He must be insane. Why on earth would anyone let go of such an opportunity?*

Turned out, he had no one outside; he begged to stay because here he had food, water and a place to sleep. I felt pity; I was already thinking of ways to help these prisoners when I was out.

Over time, I started to believe that I might just lose my mind over here. However, there was one thing that brought light again. That ignited the fire of hope inside of me. During the Christmas period, my mum came to visit me. She came with my stepdad. It was my court date, the same as usual. I got ready, sat in the van and headed towards the court.

The moment I stepped out of my van, I saw my mother standing with my stepfather beside my lawyer, Taraq Sayed. I cannot explain the outburst I had. For a second, the guards thought I might be trying to escape, but it was a sudden reaction. The moment I saw her, I ran towards her and hugged her intensely.

You say you've grown up and can deal with life on your own, but in your weakest moments, you're automatically going to want to run towards your guardian.

The feeling was mutual; my mum was probably more emotional at that moment. We can never compare a mother's love with ours. We cannot even measure the amount of genuine and pure love she has for us. My mum hugged me tighter than I hugged her. At that short moment, nothing mattered. I was complete. I had everything. We said so much with just expressions, tears and emotions. I had planned to vent out when I met her in person rather than over the phone because that would have broken her heart and worried her even more.

But I didn't even feel the need to use words to explain anything I felt or was going through.

I wish it could last a little bit longer, but I was called in for my case. But my mum waited for me. She stood there in anticipation, desperate to see me come out of that door so that she could hug me again. I came out, and she hugged me again. My mother has always been this emotional. Her love is always obvious. Aren't all mothers like that? At that moment, I felt everything fall back into place. I forgot I was a prisoner, that too, for a crime I did not commit.

Unfortunately, that moment didn't last long, as I was pulled away. The guards weren't bad people; they were just doing their job. We didn't like them because, well, they made sure we didn't break the rules. And as a prisoner, who wouldn't want to do that?

But at that moment, the guards felt something; maybe they saw a mother's unconditional love, maybe they saw a reflection of their mother's love. Maybe one of them didn't have a mother anymore to hug them. What an agony that must be, a life without a mother…or maybe they could understand that I was in for something I did not do. Maybe their experience made them capable enough to detect innocence.

Anyway, they decided to give us 10 minutes to talk and then said I had to go to the lock-up to eat lunch. The court has a café so you can buy food from there. I asked the guard if I would be coming back, and he said 'Yes'.

I told mum and Alf, my stepfather, I would see them in 20 minutes or so. Halfway through eating lunch, the prison van came, and I was told to get on. After begging and pleading and trying to explain that I had not said goodbye to my family, they still pushed me into the van. I was so upset imagining mum waiting for me and nobody to tell her I'd gone back to jail. I was shouting and punching the van roof; luckily, the French lad was in also, and he calmed me down. I was just relieved that mum and Alf got a visit for 15 minutes at the prison a few days later, so I could explain what had happened. The visit is across a 2-metre gap with wired mesh as windows, so although it was nice to see them, it wasn't long enough, and of course, no hugs to say goodbye to.

I remember times when I used to tease her; God knows how many times I've made her worried or made her cry. No matter how much I do for her, I believe I can never give her back enough. I also believe that this effort she made was powerful enough to save my life, even though it was just for minutes because I was gradually losing hope. I was losing options to hold on to. I was unfortunate enough not to understand that I have my mother's love holding on to me, making sure I do not fall. And even if I fell, I knew now that there was someone stronger than me waiting to catch me.

A fearless person isn't always a person with nothing to lose; it is often a person who has a mother behind his back, making sure she never loses him.

That night, I slept fearlessly.

After my mum went back to Manchester, she sent money through the British Embassy; it was £200, with which I could have £20 per month (1500 rupees deposited in my PPC account). This was my first payment. The embassy also bought me some clothes and bathing items with my money.

After a couple of days of boredom and living the same routine, someone told me there was another English guy in the no. 1 barrack. He told me that the English guy worships in the communal building on Sundays.

I was eager to meet someone from my homeland, so I waited for the next Sunday.

Finally, Sunday arrived, and I met him at the church.

'Hey mate'! I said.

'Uh, hello! I'm Mick from Blackburn'.

'I'm Baz, Barry Hulse from Salford'.

We chatted for a while, and he told me he was smuggling something from Thailand, and they caught him red-handed. It was fourteen months, and his trial had still not started. It scared me a little, but I thought to myself mine is a different offence, so obviously, it will take less time, besides I've been reassured several times that it'll just take sixty days. We talked about football and other mutual interests. I could tell we would become great friends as we both enjoyed the conversation. We could relate to each other not just because of the homeland but because of the fact that we both were framed. The only difference is that he was involved, but what had to be a normal day for his shipment was actually a set-up. The other person he was involved with used him for bait.

So, every Sunday, we met and had chats about different places and different topics. Things seemed better when I became friends with him as well. Everything felt quite easier. I started to settle in; when I went into my barrack, my other friends paid for a nicer place near the wall for the bedding. I felt so relieved. I won't say things were getting better because I was still in prison. But at least things were getting bearable. I no longer considered every second as torture. I did not really want to change my barrack, though I had finally adjusted. Besides, there were mostly old men here who didn't seem dangerous to me. I wasn't looking for a change until one night before Christmas....

After another restless night and bad dreams, I woke up around 2 AM. I looked around; it was winter and chilly, and all I could see were 220 bodies under white sheets. I panicked, thinking I was in a morgue and I had woken up after being dead.

As Christmas passed, I requested to be moved to the no. 1 barrack to be with another British man, and this was sanctioned in the mid of January.

The no. 1 barrack was quite cleaner and a lot smaller than 8 no. It was one building with two cells with between eight to ten men in each. It had cleaner toilets, and as soon as I entered, I noticed how quiet it was as there were only twenty prisoners. People used to get up in time for exercise and meditation as there was space to roam around the barrack and also a covered area where you could wash clothes or shower. I felt I had made the right decision to transfer here.

The best thing about this barrack was that the people there were educated. You could tell by the way they greeted you, smiled at you and minded their own business, especially by how they kept their belongings. Mick had a ludo board as well.

The most unusual thing about barrack no. 1 was that there was a person named Mustafa Dossa in there. Mustafa Dossa was basically in for the Mumbai bomb attacks. He was under trial for a complete conspiracy. However, he was quite powerful inside the prison as well. One building was just for him. He had people waiting for his order; it was terrifying, to be honest. Every Muslim in jail used to get clothes and food at festivals from him.

People respected him; he literally had the power to make things work. His word was basically everybody else's command. People didn't realise it, but I guess underneath all that respect was fear and terror, mainly because Mustafa Dossa was a terrorist and had links with the underworld.

To further explain, the Mumbai bombings were a series of twelve bomb blasts that took place on the 12th of March 1993 in Mumbai, which was known as Bombay at that time in India. It was a very severe terror attack that wasn't just a shock to India but went across the world as shocking news. There were two hundred above casualties and over seven hundred injuries.

I also remember the day it all came in the news. It moved me to the core. In the afternoon, around 1:30, a bomb went off, which was powerful enough to destroy buildings and kill over fifty people. Approximately thirty minutes later, another car bomb went off, and this went on for two hours. Killing over three hundred-plus people in a single day.

Mustafa Dossa is considered the mastermind of these attacks. He was called 'Bhai', which is a word Indians use for respect or to acknowledge someone's power, not to forget that he had ties with someone who is still somewhere free and wanted by Interpol: the mafia don Dawood Ibrahim.

However, the officials were always after Mustafa Dossa. They suspected him of running a gang from inside the prison as well. But Mustafa being powerful never got caught. I saw him do things other prisoners weren't allowed to do. Like he used to smoke marijuana inside the prison, too.

This was certainly the opposite world for me. I could never imagine being in the same room with someone who killed over 300 people. I mean, I wouldn't even want to hurt a fly.

How do people do this? How can one sleep at night knowing they destroyed someone's life? If I hurt someone, I am reminded of it in everything I do. Even if I laugh at a random joke, I quickly go on a guilt trip, thinking I took this away from them. What if they don't laugh anymore?

Are you not aware of how the world works? Whatever you do, comes back to you. Even if it's a simple compliment or an insult, beware because it will come back to you.

How do you get to the point of being so brutal? So inhumane? What do you have to kill inside you to be able to kill someone else?

I guess these narrations in my mind were enough to keep me engaged through these weeks. And eventually, the time passed by.....

Chapter
Five

Your mind refuses to accept, but at the same time, your body learns to adapt.

You hold on to the rope of hope expecting it to lead you somewhere safe, but what you don't see is that the weight of your fate is much heavier until, of course, the rope breaks.

What's worse than being hit by a gravitational force of sadness? Simple: Being hit by a stronger force of disappointment.

Call it torment, agony or injustice; I somehow managed to pass these sixty days. I remember losing count of the days in between. This was probably when I made friends.

Friends are important. Their presence can turn a horrific event into an adventure, and their absence can turn a celebration into a disappointment.

I am glad I made good friends there, people who managed to not just keep me going but turn my torment into an adventure.

The clearest memory I have of that time was when I was talking to this one prisoner; he was telling me how he had dreams and goals. I thought to myself, *Mate, you're in prison!*

But I guess it didn't really matter to him. What stood out was the light in his eyes. He was genuinely excited about his dreams. I could see that if he got the chance, he would certainly take it seriously.

The most beautiful moment is when people talk about their passion; you can see their eyes light up with hope, their posture giggles up with excitement, and there's just so much honesty and positivity in their vibe at that moment.

I had felt the same a couple of times before this tragedy happened. Although nobody ever mentioned it to me, I knew what it was like. I was always the kind of person who never had enough. When I got what I worked hard for, I worked harder for something else.

What is the point of life after you have achieved your goals? So, I continued creating further goals and achieving them. I always wanted my son to learn this from me. If not anything, then at least this. But at that point, I didn't really know what he'd think of me.

Sometimes, I thought I had failed him. Even though I was just a victim, I know this must be affecting him somehow.

I believe love is the most beautiful feeling in the world. But it brings along a lot of drawbacks. One of the most common drawbacks is this particular connection; you are bound to feel what they feel. So, if they're happy, you're happy. But if they're hurt, so are you.

I knew my son must be sad. He must be having unanswered questions invading his mind. I used to put him to bed; he must be missing my warm hug and the way I used to tuck him in.

I was a little lost in between until I realised my freedom was almost around the corner. Sixty days were about to be over soon.

Several thoughts came rushing in. I started imagining the day I got out. I had even planned to surprise my son. My friends in prison were already prepared to see me go. I could tell as they started their conversations with, 'We'll miss you in here. Now, who's going to do this when you're gone'?

The best thing about these people was that nobody was pretending; there wasn't any agenda behind any of their actions. What you'll see would be the exact reality. So, I could tell they were genuinely happy for me. I remember this one person asking me if I'd write letters to him after I was out. I felt a bit sad. I mean, I do not support whatever they did that landed them there, but I believed these were just people unaware of the consequences or just good people with bad habits. I really hoped for them to be out soon like me.

I was ready to put it all past me; I just waited there anxiously for the day to come. I counted and reassured myself. The exact date of my freedom was the 19th of January.

Every night the ticking of the clock was like a pound on my chest. I had stopped sleeping again. But this time, it wasn't the cause of fright; I just wanted to go to sleep in my own bed now. It was as if there was this fire inside me that could only be put out once I was out of there.

I had planned to buy some gifts for my son since I wouldn't be able to explain to him my entire situation. I was willing to do anything to make it up to him. I was getting impatient, to be honest. I was craving to get out of these walls, get on a plane and breathe the air of my homeland.

People noticed me zoning out in the middle of the conversations. It was almost as if I was daydreaming. I remember we were all sitting on the floor and having conversations while somebody asked me something. I was staring at him point blank, but my mind was somewhere else.

They pulled me out of my imagination and laughed out loud. I found it funny too. But what they didn't know was that I was zoned into my future, the future that is just days after.

I imagined myself getting off the plane. My mother was right there waiting for me. The moment I saw her, I ran. I ran as fast as I could, and I hugged her. The imagination was so intense that I actually felt like I had hugged her.

I had experienced all these emotions before; love, pain, excitement and fear. But the intensity I felt in prison, I would never have experienced otherwise.

I guess this was an experience that taught me things I would never have learnt in any other situation. I also believe I met the right people in the wrong place. Maybe this was a lesson for something that waits for me ahead. Maybe there is a greater meaning behind everything that happened.

There is always more to the story. Nothing in this world is ever meaningless; even a tiny step has a purpose to it.

While I was busy planning my future, I got called into the superintendent's office. While approaching the office, I felt overly excited. This was just a day or two before the 19th of January. I thought to myself, *They must be calling me in to instruct me on how to leave prison. I mean, there must be some rules.*

Anyway, I approached the superintendent's office, and there stood an officer right in front of me. His expressions were a bit confusing; they showed mixed feelings like fear, embarrassment and disappointment. In short, it was pretty clear this wasn't a face to spread some good news. I gulped and gasped for breath. I had a negative vibe that made my heart sink. I didn't understand anything at that moment until he spoke, '*Mr Barry, I would like to inform you that your investigation has been prolonged to ninety days'*.

To be precise, the moment I heard this was the moment I felt my heart was sliced in half. I actually felt the hurt physically. His words cut right through me. It was like I was walking on glass, and now the glass had broken. I was hanging in thin air, speechless, just staring at the person who didn't just break the worst news to me but broke my heart as well.

Sometimes, happiness just isn't meant for you

Chapter
Six

Have you ever been in a situation where news broke to you, and it shifted something inside of you? Like you felt the words physically?

You want to know what's worse. Worse is when your heart is pounding with excitement, and there's this adrenaline rush in you, but all of a sudden, something hits you. Something hits you so fast that the pounding stops. There's no rush or chaos anymore. Just silence. Plain, pin-drop silence.

As soon as I was told I would not be released soon, I broke. It was like I had been running in a tunnel for sixty days, and when I finally reached the other end, when I could finally see the light, someone closed the door. This was a major disappointment for me. I literally felt like there were broken pieces of me on the floor.

'But…why'? I asked gradually, but honestly, I really didn't want to know. It was enough emotional turmoil for the day. Besides, I believed they were just dragging things. They told me my charge sheet wouldn't come for another thirty days; I really wanted the charge sheet to arrive as it contained all the evidence in one place. Since I was innocent, I knew they'd realise this the moment they saw it all on paper.

What happened after that was there was a visit from the customs. The officers looked at me and said, 'Mr Barry, we've got a third parcel…'

How worse could my life get? It was like every door opened to a new bad experience. I was craving for any good news, even the slightest, to hold on to. It turns out the third parcel contained more than 22,000 tablets of Diazepam.

It all made sense; this is why they took an extension of thirty more days…

A few years ago, if I were to think of my current situation, I would have said I'd die. I believe we are always stronger than we think...

When your life turns into a series of unfortunate events, you tend to get used to it. You slowly lose the ability to be surprised or shocked. It is kind of like you're stuck between being okay and not okay. The element of 'want' or 'desire' just disappears from inside of you.

I did not lose hope, but I gradually lost the desire to want anything. I stopped complaining. I stopped looking for answers. I was going wherever life was taking me. I didn't know if I was being tested, but I decided to test myself. There was a point where I said to myself, 'Let's see how far you can go with this'. And I kept going.

Two of my friends came to visit me in January. We spoke for hardly fifteen minutes, but it felt good mainly because we'd been friends since the age of fifteen or sixteen. I remember watching football with them at the weekends. They were the kind of friends you didn't need to vent to; they already knew how you felt. They came to the prison, all the way from England, just to see me for fifteen minutes. I could see the pain in their eyes. I could tell they weren't happy to see me like this. They informed me about my mother's call. My mother called everyone she knew for help and support. It broke my heart a little when I heard this; I realised she was as desperate as me. Maybe more. Anyway, they comforted me and left.

Hope comes in different ways, sometimes through a person who is hoping as much as yourself.

Days passed, and I was hit with more bad news. I was told the charge sheet wasn't being produced yet because the investigation was still ongoing; therefore, it would take a total of 180 days. It didn't quite surprise me this time. I just looked at them, sighed and said, 'Alright…'

I didn't even think about my situation in my head. I just wanted to ignore all the bad news and continue living the way I had to until I got released. And so I did.

In March, my mum came over again, and this time she brought along my son. As soon as I was told they were here to see me, I got anxious. I didn't want my son to see me like this. I never wanted this for him. But, on the other hand, I was equally desperate to see him. I went to the visiting area, but with the bars and distance separating us, I obviously could not hug him. I put a smile on my face and acted like I was in good spirits, although I just wanted to somehow get through the screen to the other side and hug him. If only that was possible. I told my son that if he paid 1,000 rupees as a bribe, which was like £10 or £12 pounds at that time, he could get an extra ten minutes to chat with me. So, he did. It felt quite satisfying after meeting them as it brought back all the memories. They both were emotional too. I felt like my son had a lot to say to me, but we didn't have the time.

My lawyer Taraq Sayed applied for my bail in January 2010, which was rejected on the grounds of the charge sheet not being produced. He knew it would be rejected, but he did it anyway because my family was pressurising him. He tried again in April, but it again got rejected.

I was in the No.1 barrack from January till April 2010. It was still hell but the best area within the prison. Mick and I also got half a big mac, a slice of pizza and even ice cream on different days during this period provided by Mustafa Dossa. To taste good food was an absolute privilege and really helped with my state of mind. I was in a routine, breakfast, exercise for two hours (Mustafa had weights), play Ludo, read papers or books and laugh at jokes with Mick. I was still in hell but felt like I had a slice of heaven.

For the eight court dates I had over this period, I only had guard escorts on two occasions. The "*Guard Problem*", as everyone called it, was because there were too many prisoners and not enough guards to accommodate. My grandson was born on 1st March as a 36-year-old grandfather and received many cards, letters and photos. It hurt not being there, but I was keeping things together mentally. Then, the last week in April, disaster struck; the building we were in had cracks everywhere and was to be demolished. The superintendent offered each of us a choice of which barrack we preferred to transfer to. All the barracks were overcrowded, so Mick and I opted for the Anda Barrack. This was sanctioned, and we moved in on 2nd May 2010, which was also my birthday.

The Anda Barrack was for high-profile or especially dangerous prisoners; mostly, those facing terror charges were kept in specialised barracks such as the Anda barrack. It was a circular stone structure. They call it a prison within a prison. It had a lookout tower in the centre and had 4 separate areas, including Area 5, which is next to the entranceway where all the guards sit. Area numbers 1 and 4 had six cells in each, and numbers 2 and 3 had nine cells. Each cell is 4 x 15 ft., and a walkway of a couple of feet wide along each cell, all of these areas were almost the same in structure. The tower at the centre had glass windows at the top so the guards could look into each cell.

All the areas in the Anda Barrack were vacant at present, as a bombproof barrack was finished being built to house a terrorist from Anda Barrack, a well-known criminal all around the world; a terrorist, a murderer and a person who at just the age of 20 sent chills down the world's spine.

Ajmal Khasab, the lone surviving terrorist who attacked Mumbai with five associates on 26th November 2008 and continued his brutality for four days, killing and wounding hundreds of innocent people.

I felt sick knowing he would have occupied my cell at one time.

Anyway, on 20th May, the charge sheet came. I was charged with the export of three cartons of drugs. There was a total of 75,100 tablets. They further accused me of being linked with a gang. It was like they were conspiring against me.

I met a few Muslim guys in the Anda barrack; they were highly knowledgeable when it came to Indian law. I started sitting with them to understand my case a bit more, perusing my charge sheet and looking for any technicalities or loopholes in the case. It turns out they were involved in the bomb blast in 2006. They were all educated and respectful, so we got along fine. We were all assigned our own cells with 24-hour running water available, so taking 4–5 showers helped with 40 degrees plus heat and humidity.

Gradually, I sort of became numb. It really didn't make a difference because nothing was happening anyway. So, I stopped reacting much to the news and hopes they were giving me from time to time.

In the month of June, monsoon season starts, and although it's a respite from the heat, it brings along other problems. In India and many other countries, monsoon season is sort of a mosquito season. I ended up contracting malaria 5 times over the following four months. I remember I was in low spirits; it was horrific at that time. I used to shiver; I had severe headaches, vomiting, pain in the abdomen, nausea and even diarrhoea. I don't remember being this sick ever before. As soon as the authorities realised my condition was severe, they took me to the barrack hospital. I was put on a metal frame bed which had a two-inch thick mattress. It was disgusting; I saw mites crawling and stains all over it. I was close to tears, just thinking if I could go home and be looked after. I wanted someone who genuinely cared for me at that time. They weren't even treating me properly; the only medication I was on was paracetamol. Two days of being a patient of malaria made me think I was about to die. I had trouble breathing as well. On the third day, I got some strength and managed to get up and move around.

We're told we come alone and we die alone, but what about the time in between? That's when we really need someone...

Looking at my condition now, I realise the first time I got malaria, it was very severe. I got it again after a few weeks, and that's when I realised it wasn't as bad as the first time. The next three times I had it, I stayed in my cell and shook it off after two days; I think my immune system learnt to fight it. I lost 5–6 kilos over this time, not entirely because of malaria, though; maybe it was a combination of the food and stress as well.

My family came over to see me again in August. I mentioned to mum I was sick, but I didn't want to worry her, so I just showed her I was okay. My mother was genuinely concerned about the lawyer I had hired,

Taraq Sayed. Even though I knew he was trying his best, they doubted his expertise or intentions. She kept on saying I needed a new lawyer because, clearly, he didn't get me anywhere. The reason I chose Taraq Sayed was that he was one of the best NDPS lawyers there was in India.

Before mum came for the prison visit, she had met with a lawyer named Majeed Memon. He was recommended by an organisation called *Fair Trials International.* FTI is based in London and supports ensuring that British prisoners get a *FAIR TRIAL* in less liberal countries. He was a noted criminal lawyer with a high success rate in big cases. He told my mum that for £15,000, he would get me out. My friend had sold my car for me, and mum got the rest of the money together. Everyone was desperate, so the decision was made, and I came to find out about the visit, which gave me more hope. My mother helplessly requested him to reduce his fees, but he apparently acted like a salesperson instead of a lawyer.

My heart breaks, my heart breaks because everything has become a business now. Where is the sentiment of humanity? Where was the time when people genuinely wanted to help someone?

My sister Lindsay organised a fundraiser in a social club the month before they came, and this also raised a few thousand. Friends and family donated things to bid on or to be raffled off. A cousin and a close friend also had their chest and eyebrows waxed for donations. Mum brought along all the photographs from that night; there were enlarged photographs on canvas of me and everybody kissing it and holding bottles of beer to my lips. It was a big boost knowing all the love and support were there, and I was gone but not forgotten.

When we honestly ask ourselves which person in our lives means the most to us, we often find that it is those who, instead of giving advice, solutions, or cures, have chosen rather share our pain and touch our wounds with a warm and tender hand.

This life is what you make it. No matter what, you're going to mess up sometimes; it's a universal truth. But just remember, during this period, some people may come, and some may go. The ones that stay with you through everything—they're your true well-wishers. It gave me strength to have somebody to fight for, some people around me who wanted to fight for me. Life is far more than anything you can ever see or hear, or touch. It's about love that conquers hate, a peace that rises triumphant over war, and justice that proves more powerful than depravity; these are the kind of things without which humankind cannot survive.

For the next three months, everything was the same. The same routine, the same food and the same people to talk to. The only time I had fun was when I was introduced to this board game called the Carom board. It was a fun game, and a lot of people there were always enthusiastic about it.

Anyway, I realised I was becoming a bit dull, so I decided to exercise every morning; it kept my muscles from aching. Besides, there's one more thing I remember; clearly, I met a person who was shifted in mine and Mick's cell for a while as there had to be three people. I don't remember his name correctly, but we called him *Bo*; he was involved in the 1999 aeroplane hijack.

Meeting people like these wasn't exciting; it was quite scary, I'll tell you. I never imagined I'd be among people so merciless and dangerous. Even though they were inside the prison, they were still quite powerful. It was clear as I saw people lowering their tone in front of him and making sure they didn't say anything wrong.

Maybe people like these liked it. They liked the power; they liked how people were afraid of them. To them, it didn't really matter if they were imprisoned or sentenced to death; all that mattered was that they affected people around them.

If you can't make them love you, make them dread you.

On 24th December 1999, an Indian Airlines was en route to Delhi from Nepal when it got hijacked. It was all over the news. It wasn't a normal hijacking where a plane was forced to land somewhere else just to negotiate their demands; it was well-planned and constructed. The hijackers belonged to a terrorist organisation, and their demands were to release well-known terrorists who were involved in great massacres. The plane landed at several places, and the Indian government couldn't succeed. Bo was a Muslim from Punjab.

Meeting him is a memory I can't forget.

Majeed Memon finally applied for my bail, which was now applicable because my charge sheet had arrived. But the problem was that there was a rule that if you carry under 500 grams of Diazepam, it falls under commercial, which means the maximum sentence you'll get would be ten years. And if it exceeds the commercial limit, god knows for how long you'll be stuck in there. I was so anxious when Majeed Memon broke this news to me; I was worried if I'll ever be able to live with my family again. Because the amount I was charged was over 751 grams equalling 75,100 tablets.

You never really value time until you start to lose it.

So, he argued for bail, and since he was such a big name in the game, he got me bail from the same judge who had rejected it twice before. The bail was agreed at 150,000 rupees, which was 75,000 as surety and 75,000 as solvency. This was £2,000 as per the exchange rate at the time. Solvency and surety are basically a guarantee from someone who stands for you so you don't run away. I was okay with it; I mean, I'd do anything to get out of there. But, the prosecutor argued that I shouldn't be given bail since my charge was above the commercial limit. The judge then decided to give me a two-week stay, which allowed the prosecution to file against the decision in the high court. Anyway, we paid the money and waited for two weeks.

At that time, I thought another Christmas period was coming, and I needed to get out of there. I can't celebrate Christmas away from my family again. Since I was going outside on bail, I was thinking of escaping from the country. Because, by now, I realised that I shouldn't trust anyone here anymore. Anything could happen, and since I had finally got a chance to breathe outside the prison for a while, I didn't want it to end.

So, I waited...

Another Christmas passed, and a new year was just around the corner.

A new year is always expected to be the beginning of a new life, a fresh new start.

Little did I know this New Year would be the beginning of everlasting torment for me.

Every time you face an unpleasant situation, you believe this is the worse you've ever been through until the worst walk in your life.

Chapter Seven

While we worry about how time will pass by, time does pass by. And it does so very quickly.

I was obviously anxious over the Christmas period waiting on any news of my bail, listening every day to the loudspeaker hoping I would hear my name, but it never came. I got no guards for my court date, but the second week in January, Mick went to court, and Taraq Sayed told him he heard my bail had been cancelled by the high court the day before. Mick brought the news to me when he came back; I was devastated, I felt empty, and all my plans for outside had evaporated.

A week later, I had a visit from Majeed Memon's junior, who told me they were going to the supreme court in Delhi to fight the decision. I asked him would £17,000 cover this, but he said it would cost more. I didn't want to waste more time and money on an uncertain outcome, so I declined and told him to tell Mr Memon to try and start the case proceedings instead. I knew at that point I was in for at least another year!

During the January to May period, I had no guards for court. It's nice to break the monotony and see the outside world, so this, combined with what was happening after my bail was rejected, was a really difficult period. When I finally got guards in May, I was met by Majeed Memon and his entourage at court. He told me he didn't want to do my case anymore because of constant pressure from my family, British Embassy and FTI via email and phone. I was pleased because I didn't want him to represent me anymore anyway; I felt he wasn't interested now that he had his money. I asked him about the money we paid, and he said he would speak with my family about it as he was going to London in August and would meet mum then. I didn't hold much hope.

I passed my time over this period relatively easily as I had Mick to talk to. There were also two Mexicans and a Venezuelan who was in my area for the theft of nearly £1 million worth of diamonds. They were professional thieves who would travel the world in their occupation, so they were "*street smart*" and educated. They spoke Spanish but understood some English, and we had some good banter together and became good friends over the few months they were there. Taraq Sayed got an acquittal for Mick in the first week of July, and then a week later, the three diamond thieves' friends were convicted for 21 months. This was only if they paid back over a *million dollars*, which they did, and all the diamonds were recovered. They did a plea agreement with the defendant, which means you plead guilty and serve only a quarter of the sentence. They got seven years, so they had to do 21 months. With these people gone, time started to drag again.

As Taraq had got Mick acquitted, I decided to retain him again to fight my case. In August 2011, my judge got changed, and Taraq got my case charged and framed before him that month. A charge frame is basically when the judge accepts all pieces of evidence and a list of witnesses etc., that will be involved in the trial. Mick was still in Mumbai as he had to stay for an extra 3 months until the prosecution decided whether to appeal against his acquittal in the high court. He was posting my letters and visiting me, and I helped him with money for accommodation and food etc. On one court date in November, my first witness was produced, and the judge was giving me every 10-day date and not 14. Taraq told me he would get me out within three months. Things were starting to look up.

The worst is when you're left hanging, not knowing if you'll fall or land on the ground.

In December 2011, I was introduced to someone who changed the rest of my days at Arthur Road Prison. He was hiding in Bangkok and was connected with Dawood Ibrahim. He was caught and extradited back to India to face assorted charges. He was appointed my area in the number-two section. I noticed he had his own cell, and he was locked in for two weeks.

Later, I came to know someone was trying to kill him. It was a threat for him to be locked up with people or to just be around them. Because he once worked for the most-wanted man on earth: Dawood Ibrahim, but he was on his own now. They used to work altogether.

Santosh Shetty, Chhota Rajan, and Dawood Ibrahim. It was a request from his lawyer to keep him away from anyone for safety purposes. It was quite understandable because he was wanted in nine murder and extortion cases.

I was already trying to pass my time, so I decided to approach him and stand by his cell and chit-chat. To my surprise, he was polite, well-mannered and spoke English better than me. I found his conversations quite interesting as he was very knowledgeable.

One day, while we were just chatting, he told me a story about when he stayed in Thailand. Santosh told me Dawood Ibrahim had sent people to kill him and Rajan, and they managed to shoot Rajan twice. Santosh had no choice but to take his friend to the hospital. The third and fourth floor was filled with Thai guards because Chhota Rajan was a well-known gangster, and it was a delicate situation since he got shot in a gang rivalry.

What he told me next blew my mind. I thought to myself, *This isn't possible.* He said they got along well with the Thai police after a few weeks. So, when Chhota Rajan got better, they got sleeping pills and drinks for the guards, and then when they were knocked out, then they repelled down the ropes from the third-floor window to the ground. They were then picked up in a helicopter to cross the border into Burma. Not only that, they then managed to get a boat to sail over to Malaysia. I thought this was unbelievable. In my heart, I believe he was just exaggerating things. I've only seen people pulling these stunts successfully in movies.

Anyway, ironically, just a few days later, I got the English daily newspaper like I used to. I saw the front page with his picture on it. The news was about the story he told me and also that people in the film industry are thinking of making a movie about him. I thought to myself, *He's a well-connected person. I was wrong about him, he was telling the truth. He did escape from the hospital.* Since these journalists have a habit of digging deep into things, I also read about how he took lessons on rope climbing. Since he was just arrested, all his old crimes were coming up.

Moving on to 2012, we got very close. He rearranged the prison system, which was almost impossible for anyone else to do. He clearly had a lot of power. The prison usually keeps odd numbers in the cell. Like there must be one or three people in the cell and not two or four. I never really understood this rule. They feared homosexuality or fights, I think.

Because Santosh was such a big figure, he was paying money to all the officers. Gradually, when he started recognising people, he decided to come out of his cell every day.

I was in a cell with two Muslims over this time who were in for separate terrorist charges. One lad called Feroz was Mustafa Dossa's co-accused for the 1993 bombings, and the other lad, Farooq, was in for the 2006 bombings.

One morning at headcount, Farooq was ill and lay down, the guard was shouting, and Feroz told him to be quiet. Next thing, a lot of abuse was shouted at each other (I now understood approximately 5% of the language), and the guard brought back two other guards and opened our cell gate. The next thing, Feroz and I were fighting with the guards for 5 minutes until they got us back in the cell and locked up again. I had to go to the office area in the afternoon to make a statement, and the superintendent, guards responsible, Feroz, and Farooq were present. A few minutes later, Mustafa Dossa came in, and what I'd seen and heard shocked me. The superintendent was apologising, saying, '*Sorry, Bhai*'. And all the guards were saying the same. I realised who ran the prison then because any other prisoners would have been beaten up badly for that incident.

After the New Year, in Jan 2012, he requested the officers that I go in his cell with him. He had three *kaamwalas*, which was a word in Hindi used for workers. We used to have good conversations; the days were a lot quicker with him, honestly. We used to do crosswords and play Ludo as well. There was a point when I thought he had OCD (obsessive-compulsive disorder). That, too, because he used to put things in patterns and always made sure they were very clean.

After a while, he got our cell painted. Gradually, we got sugar and tea bags in and also two thermoses. There was a lot of milk coming in the morning, so *kaamwalas* used to keep the thermoses filled with tea and coffee.

We had a couple of extra covers on the floor and a couple of extra sheets as well. There were a total of four or five sheets for each, so it was enough padding on the floor to sleep peacefully. The rest of the people who were in the area for the following year were mostly policemen. In India, gangsters would pay the police to shoot their rivals. These policemen have been accused of shooting 105 people for them.

After 9 o'clock, we would sing Hindi songs for an hour, and all the nine cells in our area would join in; everybody got along really well. It was clear Santosh confided in me because he told me almost everything. Inside the prison, people spoke about their cases but avoided the details; everybody was well-guarded because nobody knew who might become a witness or what might be used against them in court. However, I finally felt like I had a really close friend after all this time.

The best thing was that the place was clean, there were no bugs or anything. And so I wasn't getting sick anymore. Santosh had a wider space to sleep in than me, but I was absolutely okay with it.

I often wonder, *What is the point of happiness if it isn't meant to last forever?*

Mid-January 2012, the judge who had finally started to work on my case was transferred to another court out of state. After which, there was complete silence for a while. Approximately for six months, there was nothing. There were hardly three judges who dealt with NDPS in India, and the cases were outnumbered. I wasn't expecting anything but silence after the judge was transferred anyway, but I also wasn't expecting to have any judge run my case for such a long period.

However, I still had a bit of contact with my family, apart from the letters that are. Whenever I went to court (which wasn't often because 70 percent of the time, there were no guards), I used to request a phone call to have a chat with my family. Going to court was a big thing on its own, not just for me but for almost every prisoner. Through those proceedings, we managed to see the world again. Even though it wasn't for a long time, it was worth it.

Meanwhile, amidst the silence, we were all getting along very well. Mostly because there were different people coming in and going out, meaning there was not enough time to bond with each other. This time, everyone was at the same place and stayed there for a longer period of time. We used to gather around and have fun in the little yard area we were provided. My routine got better than it was before. I felt more active and positive in those days. We played a game of volleyball and did some exercises as well.

Rey served 3.5 years in the trial and then got acquitted in the session court but had to remain in Mumbai for 6 months as the prosecution had appealed. Mick, however, went back home after three months. Rey's case was a bit intense as compared to anyone else's, as it was heroin.

Rey was a bit tense as he really didn't know what he'd do after he got out. Santosh needed somebody on the outside to work for him. Since I trusted him, I put in a good word, and things sorted out eventually. Rey offered to work for Santosh, and he agreed and decided to pay him £100 every month along with my £100.

I genuinely cared about him because he was one of the initial friends I made there. But obviously, there was a personal motive as well. He could bring any items I needed to court and pass on urgent messages from home etc. He could also bring me charged batteries and movies on the USB drive to smuggle back into the prison.

Life was better with Santosh, to be honest. Whenever I went to court, the officers were extra nice to me. I remember this one officer walking up to me and saying, 'So you are the English guy Santosh talks about so much'!

He was so delighted to meet me. I always wondered how did they manage to pull those emotions off, was it the money, were they afraid of Santosh, or were they genuinely happy to see someone close to him?

The food was great; Santosh had arranged a food order which allowed him to have a tiffin delivered for lunch and dinner. A tiffin is a metallic container with sections to put in various food. We had a menu from a restaurant, and I used to order 10 days' lunch and dinner in advance. Rey was working for Santosh at this point, doing all his work outside, so he used to take my food list and pick up the food from the restaurant and bring it for us twice a day to the prison. Santosh was paying the prison staff for this privilege.

I went to worship every Sunday. The Church was simply a stone area. I remember that was the time I started getting into religion more. I developed this perspective that whatever happened, happened for a reason.

It was good for me as it added more room for hope and survival through the hurdles I was facing. That phase was more of a spiritual healing for me, and I'm thankful for it still.

Anyway, they used to let me get food and stay for a longer time period. Sometimes, even for four hours, just because of Santosh, obviously. Whenever they were extra nice to me, I used to compare it to the times before. Before I met Santosh, the very same people made sure I ate in the garage and didn't spend a minute in peace. I can never forget the time I didn't even get to say goodbye to my mother. Before, their attitude towards me was the opposite; all they had to offer me was strictness and rudeness. And now, it was all gone. Now, I was Santosh's man. So they made sure I faced no inconvenience.

I spent those days at ease; everything was going well compared to whatever I had faced before, except for the fact that my case was nowhere to be heard. There were many times when I didn't even get to go to court because there were no guards, so life for me at that point was everything inside the prison, and thankfully, it was going well.

One helping hand can turn hell into a hell of a time.

Chapter Eight

You get a few things going your way, and without realising it, you have negotiated your life.

Chhota Rajan had ordered a hit by his gang. The person shot was a reporter named JD, and nine members of his gang that were involved were brought in and put in cell no. 3, which was right next to us.

As time passed by, I finally met the judge; he told me to wait two more weeks as my case would start again. This meant they were done with two witnesses, and now fourteen were left.

I, to this date, do not understand why the judge said he was going to transfer me back to the previous courtroom.

Anyway, over the next few months, the witnesses started coming in, and my case was moving forward. The witnesses were from the prosecution's side. I, however, didn't go to court every time. Sometimes, the judge wasn't there, and sometimes, it was my lawyer, and mostly the prosecutor never turned up!

The good thing was that my case was going on again, it had finally started, and the witnesses were moving along.

However, this judge didn't allow me to make a phone call. I didn't quite understand why because the judges there usually didn't care much about the calls, but this particular one just didn't allow me to make a phone call at any cost. It was almost as if he personally held a grudge against me.

Over a few months, I experienced a couple of things that led me to believe he was not on my side.

For instance, one time, I heard him talking to someone in Hindi. I obviously didn't understand what he said, but there was a line he said in which he used the word 'British Raj'. I understood where this was coming from. He hated me for the fact that the British ruled India in the past. *Raj* literally means *rule* and is derived from the ancient Sanskrit language.

He was certainly getting off on the fact that I was powerless in front of him. I felt disgusted, honestly. I asked myself how one person could just play with someone else's life. I mean, this was my life in their hands. I wondered then, *Has this man got any bias against British people?*

In around August of 2012, Santosh brought a mobile phone inside the prison. That was the time I was actually relieved and felt like a superstar. You have different ranks of officers in India, the *havaldar* is an officer with one star, and then there's a sub-inspector with two stars until the highest rank of superintendent. The sub-inspector who oversaw the Anda Barrack used to receive 20,000 rupees per month from Santosh.

On the other end, Chhota Rajan's guys gave something to the officers as well. Santosh and Rajan were still enemies, but I got along well with all of Rajan's gang and would often sit in their area and chat with them all.

I hadn't met Rajan by then but had heard about him a lot because he was also very powerful and a well-known gangster. Though I met every one of his guys and friends, I didn't get to meet him as he was hiding in Australia or Indonesia and was wanted for many crimes.

Life was pretty good at the prison, apart from the fact that there was no call from the court, but I got to contact my family through the mobile phone Santosh had sneaked in. Befriending Santosh was the best thing for me at that time. Apart from having a good friend in need, prison life no longer felt like a sentence. I got to roam around the jail. In between those days, there was an English guy from London, along with two Colombians and one Indian, who came in for the case of 30 kg of cocaine.

Honestly, the only inconvenience I was facing at that moment was that I had to charge the phone secretly. But, we managed that too from the plug of the television, which was placed in the corridor. Each area had a turn every four days, and we would have a memory stick that Rey would download loads of movies on for us. Apart from that, we were playing cards in there as well, which wasn't allowed as gambling was illegal. I literally went to every barrack and was friends with everyone because of Santosh.

I met Vijay Palande, who was a serial killer for Santosh. He was in for loads of murders. Again, because of him, I easily went to 11 no. barrack and got the charged batteries for the phone, and came back. The thing that made me feel really special and like a superstar was that everybody was searched, but I wasn't searched because of Santosh; the officers would act like they were searching me, but that was just for show.

The case was moving along pretty well too. I often asked Taraq Sayed what his thoughts were on my case, and he looked quite confident. All he used to say was, 'Just keep praying, Barry, and you'll be out soon'.

My mum was obviously fighting and trying her best; she met the MP from our area and asked her to make some calls as well. I often tried to convince her not to push herself too hard because things were going pretty well at the court, and I was expecting myself to be out soon.

I was getting dates every fourteen days, and soon enough, I realised I was halfway through my case now.

The phones, USBs for movies, and every other thing we had in there was obviously illegal. To avoid these sorts of things, there is always a random search from outside officers. They normally come early morning or just before they are going to lock you in. We used to put the mobile in a sealed bag, tape it up, and drop it in the toilet attached to strings.

Now, since Santosh, Rajan's gang and others in the Anda Barrack were paying the guards for this very reason, the two-star officer would come with guards and take away everything that was illegal before the search. And after the *jherty* (search) was over, they used to come back and return it. These people who came to search were very strict; they even brought along dogs to sniff out any drugs or things like that. The purpose of their search is usually when they have come across rumours of any gangster running things from inside the prison.

Once, the search was about to take place, and Santosh wasn't warned beforehand, so he didn't give the mobile to our two-star officer to hide. He decided to flush it with buckets of water because there was no place to hide it. But I really couldn't let that happen because I was finally connected with my family. So, I decided to hide it inside my shorts. As the officer was patting me down, I lifted my vest while pushing the mobile into my shorts.

I don't know how, but I actually got away with it.

The next few months had the same routine. The 2nd May 2013 was my 40th birthday. Santosh managed to get in a chocolate cake and vodka; on the other side, Rajan's gang had brought me a cake as well. They hated each other but didn't mind me being friends with any of them. They kept me out of the politics, maybe because I wasn't Indian, and they knew I had nothing to do with them. I used to give these people magazines in jail, which my good friend Jonny used to post for me.

With my *"Jail Status"*, I now managed to arrange all my posts to get to me unopened and uncensored. I remember the first time when these guys got to look at naked women in pictures; they were shocked and amazed. They kept on asking me how this was possible and requested to get more. In India, anything related to sex is taboo, so to see naked women was a first for most.

I got along and became friends with everyone. At first, I was wary because my instinct kept telling me I had to stay cautious as these were all murderers, but gradually after spending time with them, I realised they were people just like me; I mean, at least with me, they were.

Mustafa Dossa was in the 10 no. barrack. He was friends with Santosh, so every Sunday, we used to visit the 10 no. barrack.

The 10 no. barrack was just a small house with four cells; he got it all painted, though it was definitely well-kept. The most amazing thing was that he had a swimming pool too. We used to go and eat with him on Sundays. He used to place a big sheet on the grass area, and then, I, Santosh and a few others used to sit down and eat together. The food was amazing. This usually took place after the jail was locked down.

So, gradually, the whole jail got to know me, and I was treated more like a celebrity than a prisoner.

Even though I was having fun and liked the power for a while, I often thought to myself how much I had already missed out at home. I had spent three and a half years in jail already. I used to go away from my family for a maximum of two weeks, but I somehow survived; what agony it must have been for them.

However, in May, the last witness was called. They were giving their closing arguments, and then I was called in to give my final statement.

In India, if the prosecution thinks they are going to lose the case, they simply delay it.

So, in the middle of May, when my case was finally finished, the prosecution all of a sudden wanted to recall a witness. The witness they wanted to recall was the postmaster. The first time she came in, she didn't recognise me. Also, the place had no CCTV cameras to prove any of us right. It was a well-planned move as she was from Goa, and to bring her here again, it took them over six weeks.

However, when I went for my final statement, Taraq Sayed instructed me to just answer the questions by *no* or *I don't know.*

I didn't understand why, though. Taraq Sayed wasn't available that day, but his assistant was there. The judge began asking questions. Half of the questions didn't even make sense to me. However, I did as I was told. But, there was a question in which I couldn't hear what he had asked properly, so I said, 'Yes'?

To which the assistant quickly said, 'No! He means no, your honour'! Then, I just continued to say no to every question. In the end, the judge said he'd give his final verdict in fifteen days.

These next fifteen days were a nightmare. This was because I was hanging between whether I'll be sentenced or freed. The thoughts were messing with my mind. I was extremely anxious.

I reminded myself of the evidence that was on my side. The third parcel was sent on 10th January, and I left the country on 6th January. So, I was very hopeful. In fact, I was confident. Nonetheless, I prayed as much as I could.

Finally, the day came; it was the 5th of July, 2013. I got in the van, and again they squashed in as many people as possible. There was no place to sit even; I went all the way to court standing. I guess they put forty people in the van together. I stepped out of the van and saw Rey was there to meet me. It felt good.

However, Taraq Sayed wasn't there. So, I sat with the guards on the benches. The judge was just giving dates to a couple of prisoners. And then came my turn. The judge asked me where my lawyer was and asked me to go get him as soon as possible. I went and searched for him and found him finally in another courtroom. The judge had clearly made his decision. I could see it in his expression. He was no more looking for answers. I was nervous, to which Taraq Sayed said, 'Just pray. Let's see where this goes'.

The judge started to give out his verdict, which was something like: 'I want to congratulate you both, the opposition and the defence, as I have watched you both work, and it was a nice time we spent. Thank you also for the speed and progress you have carried along the way'.

He further talked about my case. And then added: ***'Therefore, I find the convict Barry Hulse guilty, and I sentence him to a minimum of TEN YEARS of rigorous imprisonment, with three years and eight months already served to be deducted'.***

Have you ever felt like the weight of your body just dropped down? All of a sudden, your feet don't have the power to let you stand? And you just drop. You don't fall, you drop. Because it's like some power was holding you before, and all of a sudden, it disappeared into thin air.

Sometimes, God doesn't see past your will to stand.

Chapter Nine

Therefore, I find the convict Barry Hulse guilty, and I sentence him to a minimum of ten years of imprisonment, with three years and eight months already served.

Ten years…

Ten years…

That is all I could hear. My world fell apart. There were these voices in my head that kept repeating the words "ten years", and I came to a point where I actually started hitting my head. I just wanted the voices to stop. I wanted everything to just stop right there because I needed time to process what had just happened.

Ten years? I am sentenced to ten years? I waited over three and a half years to serve another six and a half more? How could this possibly be my fate when I was innocent?

Even though it took me three years and eight months to come to this point, I believe I survived because my trial was in process, and I wasn't sentenced yet. How does this world work anyway? How was there even the slightest possibility of finding me guilty when I actually wasn't?

And I had to serve six years and four months more for a crime I did not commit?

What I thought was a pause was actually a cease. At that moment, I felt God was looking down at me, laughing. I was furious, resentful, sad, and most of all, I had lost all the hope I was holding on to.

My first reaction after processing the news was to shout at Taraq Sayed.

'Taraq! Please, tell them I am innocent! Please'!

Taraq Sayed kept convincing me that we'd fight this in the high court and we won't stop. But I had lost all the energy I had.

I kept asking myself what I'd look forward to now; all I could see was a never-ending void. That day, 5th July 2013, I gave up.

I mean, I knew the legal processes in India were a little shady and slow, but I never actually thought I'd be found guilty for something I didn't do.

I begged them to allow me one phone call. Just one, but it seemed like the judge I was pleading with was heartless. I was sentenced to ten years; I deserved a chance to break the news to my family. India is four and a half hours ahead of England, and I knew mum and family would have been huddled around the phone waiting on the decision since 4 AM. Most of all, they deserved to know! If I didn't have Santosh's phone back in prison, I really don't know what would have happened to my family, how long would they have waited to just know I was not coming home...

So, there and then, I changed. My thoughts and my approach to everything changed.

I no longer waited for something; there was no longer a push inside of me. It was just me and a spiral of emptiness.

What is life without something to look forward to? You wake up and plan your day ahead, while some wake up and curse themselves for it.

I kept thinking about my family. How will they react to this, and how will they continue to live without me? And my girlfriend? I was planning to get married; of course, she wouldn't wait around this long. How will I explain to my son that he doesn't even have to wait for me anymore, that he can carry on living without me?

Taraq Sayed offered me an option as well; he said I could transfer myself to my homeland. I was well aware of this for a long time, but doing so would mean I couldn't take advantage of filing an appeal. You can appeal in the high court or apply for the transfer; both together were not an option. The agreement takes a maximum of 18 months to finalise, which would then mean I have approximately 5 years of sentence remaining, of which I would serve 50% in an English prison. This still meant another four years, so an appeal and, hopefully, an acquittal in the high court looked even more preferable. I believed I was being punished. That was enough; I didn't want my family to suffer because of it.

I took a deep breath and said to myself, *If this is it, so be it.*

And I set foot on the journey of living a life of a prisoner, not as someone just waiting for his trial.

What do you do when you are running out of options? You stop running.

I had no other option than to accept what had been brought to my fate. So, I did. I went back to the prison and continued living how I was living before the news broke to me.

Before 5th July, I always had it in the back of my mind that I just had to be here for a little more time period, and I'll be leaving this place for good soon. But after the judgment, serving six years and four months more felt like forever to me.

Before, I was adjusting till I was released, and now it felt like I had to just…adjust.

The worst thing about all of this that haunted me every second was that I was *found guilty*. This meant that not only did I have to serve more years as a criminal behind bars, but I would also have a criminal record for the rest of my life.

Even though I spent three years and eight months waiting for my trial, I had prepared myself to consider this as an incident of my life. But now, after being found guilty, how would I look back on this after I am out? Would the word 'incident' be fair to my situation? I was wronged to a level that took away a big chunk of my life.

Sometimes, I just sat, fearing that I might just end up becoming a lost cause. My life had stopped since that day, but everyone else's had not.

But you know how a mother's love is boundless. It knows no end. She fought side by side and did everything she could. And, while this was the most beautiful thing that kept me going, it broke me a little every time.

I knew her, I knew she'd never give up, and that is what scared me. She was draining herself every day. I never imagined my mum to live such a life, and that too, because of me.

Going back to the point when the judge gave his final verdict, as I was taking time to process it, everyone else was preparing themselves for further procedures. At that moment, I was behaving like a robot; even though there was chaos and destruction inside of me, I was still responding and functioning as if nothing had happened.

When we came out of the court, I kept thinking my mum and all of my family must be waiting and wondering what was going on with me. They had to know that I would not be coming back home for a long time yet. I asked Taraq to go get me permission to make a phone call. He did as I asked. I was impatient; I just wanted to dial up the number and burst into tears. To my surprise, Taraq Sayed came back and said, 'I'm sorry, Barry, but the judge won't allow you a phone call'!

I was furious. I raised my voice and said, 'What? They won't allow me a phone call? They've given me ten years, Taraq! My family deserves to know! You want to punish me, it's fine. Punish me! But don't punish my family'!

I thought to myself, *After all, these are the people who suffer the most in these situations.*

Taraq Sayed told me to calm down and said, ‘We’ll figure something out’.

Luckily, I remembered that Santosh had a phone in prison. That is when I actually calmed down. Otherwise, I don’t know what I would have done; maybe I panicked or screamed or attacked the judge. I don’t understand this, though; what would he have lost if he had given me one phone call? Nobody’s family should suffer.

On the other hand, the embassy and Rey were at the court for me as well. They kept asking me what they should tell my mum, and I managed to convince them not to say anything. This was news that they deserved to know through me so that we could mourn together.

Family isn’t to support you when you’re sad; in a family, you all mourn together.

However, my day at the court had not ended yet. I still had some procedures to follow, which included fingerprints and filling out assorted paperwork. It was standard procedure, which took a lot of hours, though. In those hours, the thought of my family waiting and wondering what might be happening kept haunting me.

After everything was done and dusted, they finally told me I was ready to go back to prison. On my way back, in the same squashed van, I kept wondering in the prison if everything would be the same for me now. However, what remained my first priority was to reach the prison and get ahold of that phone and break the news to my family. Ironically, the doctor offered me Diazepam to help me sleep when I reached the prison. For me specifically, that is. At first, I wondered what they had planned for me now. But it turns out it was standard procedure to just check on how I was doing or handling the news.

The first person I phoned was my mum, and I remember my voice was breaking, but I promised myself I would keep myself together for my family. I could not let them suffer anymore. So, as soon as I told her I was found guilty and sentenced to ten years, I added, '...but there's another way out, so there's no need to worry'!

Regardless, my mum broke down. I stayed on the phone for ten minutes as she kept crying. Santosh was guarding and looking out for any officers in sight. I spoke to my girlfriend as well; we both didn't know where we stood from there onwards and how this relationship would work further. I could feel her dreams shatter; she cried a lot. I didn't even have the power to soothe her at that moment because I myself wasn't sure of what these years ahead had planned for me.

After all, ten years is a long time.

'Child, don't wait until it's too late. Lost time is lost forever'.

— **Sonali Dev,** *A Bollywood Affair*

Chapter Ten

T*he sands of time look back at you and wonder who suffers more. Is it time; cursed for passing by, or the one it's passing for?*

Looking at the ceiling of bricks and cement, my thoughts kept pacing back and forth as I lay down that night. It was a different feeling, something in between feeling everything and feeling nothing at all. Even though I had so much on my mind, I was still blank.

I was struggling between hope and acceptance. Some days, I was hopeful of finding a way out of this mess. But other days, I remember consoling myself with the speed of time. Instead of just reminiscing about the good times, I might as well just enjoy my time here, as I had good people around me, and I was now familiar with everything.

The more you sense pain, the more time slackens down.

Hence, I sustained living a life I did not deserve, but this time, it didn't really matter. Each time a meteor hit my universe, I thought there could never be a greater collision than this, but I was proved wrong consecutively. It was almost as if the entire country had been plotting against me, as if it was their sole purpose to bring me down. So, whenever they noticed my grounds didn't break, they planned for me a finer earthquake.

And this time was no different either…

I had started wearing a uniform. Once you're convicted, you're made to wear white cotton trousers with white cotton, buttoned-up sort of shirt with yellow stripes on each arm. The yellow stripes were specifically to indicate that you are a convicted prisoner and that, too, for seven or more years. From wearing Nike and other brands to that specific uniform which was nothing less than a humiliation for me, it felt like they took my life away.

At that time, I felt devastated. The round would come every week; the superintendent would walk around with all the other officers and ask if any of us had any problems. The purpose of those rounds was to know if any prisoner wanted to place a request for letters, as it required a proper procedure or any problems and issues inside the prison regarding anything.

After my conviction, it wasn't just me who was disappointed; the people around me were equally gutted for me. Everyone in the jail knew what had happened. The word spread out like wildfire, and everyone was affected by it. If not being thwarted for me, they were definitely petrified for themselves. They had been awaiting their trial and were now fearing conviction. Everyone I spoke to either consoled me or told me they were scared for themselves.

However, the day after my conviction, I was still in the middle of processing this new lifestyle when a friend of mine in prison said, 'I really can't believe they gave you twenty years'.

I corrected him. I said, 'No, *Bill*, they have given me ten years'.

I didn't really understand why he would mistake ten for twenty, so I asked him the source. To my surprise, he said he had read it in the newspaper with the heading, '*British Man Gets Twenty Years Sentence'.*

I couldn't just ignore this, so I went and got the judgment copy. I was impatient and anxious, and I had to be sure.

I remember tapping my foot anxiously and skimming through the document until I reached the line where it said: '…sentence of ten years for export and ten years for possession'.

My eyes, like a camera lens, zoomed into the "*and"* in that sentence and stopped right there. I asked myself if this was really what it looked like.

I scrutinised the whole judgment copy and confirmed that the 2 x 10-year sentences were to run consecutively and not concurrently; I was given ten years for one charge and a further ten years for the second charge.

To rub more salt into my wounds, there was a fine of £1,400 for each sentence as well. And if in case I don't pay, I would have to serve an extra two years for each sentence as a punishment.

So, basically, I was given 24 years imprisonment…

From not being able to accept the seven more years that I had to serve in this dungeon, I had to now prepare myself for 16 more years or 20 more if I couldn't pay the fine.

Don't show the world you're happy, the devil may notice you!

My mates felt down for me; I could see they weren't as joyful as they normally were. After conviction, mum said she was coming for a visit, and this happened around the mid of July 2013. She wanted to meet me as soon as I broke the news to her. She was equally devastated, or maybe more. We always underestimate the love our mothers have for us. We never truly can measure it, can we?

Before she landed on the soil of India, I made arrangements with the doctor and the administration in the jail. I wanted to go to the JJ Hospital, which is the main hospital in Mumbai. The thing is, the doctor refers you to go to a certain hospital if you're sick. The staff in the office make arrangements which include the escorts that take you to the hospital.

If you pay, you are a priority. I told him I wanted to go to JJ as my mum was coming the following week. I asked him to make sure I got to go there at least four times in this period. I paid £150 for it as well. I gave the staff £100 to arrange the guards. I went to the hospital and met mum, who came along with my stepfather. Rey was there too; he was in contact with my family and me. He made sure that mum and Alf were comfortable in the hotel and would help them in Mumbai and going to JJ Hospital, etc. The arrangement included £50 per day as well for all the guards. Fortunately, I got to spend 3 to 4 quality hours at the hospital with mum and Alf for three days that week.

In the meantime, we were obviously looking for a way out. I would rather wait and appeal in the high court against conviction than have myself transferred to my homeland. I was also in coordination with Santosh. He told me about a very good lawyer who worked in parole.

Apparently, when you are convicted, you can get out on parole for 60 to ninety days, but you have to provide all the paperwork for it, which includes proof and reasons on why you do you need parole and whom you would meet when you are granted one. I was quite convinced by this idea. So, we arranged the lawyer and paid some money to arrange a visit with him at the superintendent's office. His name was Gawankar; I met him there with my mum, stepfather and Santosh. He assured me that he would get me out on parole, but it wouldn't be easy. However, he had a plan in his mind; one of my family members would have to come to India and stay at the hospital while he prepared a police report.

After he had submitted the police report, some officers would come to see my family member at the hospital to verify the relationship and sickness. The plan sounded a bit twisted at first, but I knew I had no other ladder to climb, so I went for it. Gawankar said he would get all the paperwork needed for the parole but wanted £2,000 for it. Since there was still some hope…I arranged it all. I said to myself, *This lawyer will get me out one way or another.*

So, we agreed that my stepfather and my son Kyle would come over at some point in the next few months. The following three weeks after that, I was able to console everyone to keep fighting and that there was hope, I had a phone on me, so I stayed in contact with everyone.

I had a strong feeling about this; I knew in my heart that this plan would work and that I would get out.

When you shake hands with the devil, the devil laughs back at you.

One Saturday afternoon, at around 2 PM, in the first week of August, some three-star officers came in and said I and a few others would be moved out from Arthur Road, as in transferred. This was because Arthur Road mostly had prisoners awaiting trial, and I, along with a few others, were now convicts serving our sentences. They told me I would be transferred to *Kolhapur Prison,* which was a 12-hour drive. I didn't want to go at all.

In fact, the only thing that kept me going at that moment was that I was familiar with everyone and everything here. I even tried telling the guards I was sick, but it didn't really matter to them. I was worried that everything, the phone, the TV, and every sort of comfort that I was privileged with, would be snatched away.

I stood my ground; I was sure they'd figure something out. But I, to this date, do not know why Santosh came in and said, 'You will have to do this for me and for my respect. They won't drag you out, but the van won't go nowhere until you get on it'.

That is when I set myself loose; the man did everything he could for me, so I listened to him. What made me anxious was the fact that I was going into the unknown again; I would have to start all over. Here, I had my place, and everyone knew me. In my heart, I really didn't want to go, but for Santosh, I started packing my belongings.

So, off you go to a road unknown

Fearing the beasts you last fought alone

In Kolhapur, you have to wear an all-white uniform as it's a rule, but once you are in your barrack, you can wear anything, so this is one thing I found quite civil.

While I was packing my belongings, I convinced myself that everything was going to be alright and I'll adjust myself there too. You know when you keep telling yourself a lie, your mind starts to believe it? So, I tricked myself just like that. Meanwhile, my mum bought me loads of new white clothes like shorts, vests and underwear and a large towel, so I was prepared for the new prison.

Finally, that day came, and I bid farewell to everyone. It was quite emotional because I had finally made some real friends.

When it's real, it's hard to say goodbye.

I got in the van, and while everyone else was settling in, or should I say being squashed in, I looked at Arthur road for the last time. I looked at it the same way I did on the day I was brought there. I noticed the paint wearing off from the sides of the buildings and the bricks with cracks on them, and I even remembered the rain in the monsoon that would leak through the cell ceilings, drip, drip, drip. The engine started, and I realised a big chapter of my life had ended, and what waited ahead for me made me apprehensive. After my conviction, everything just happened so fast; this was just four weeks after the trial was heard.

It was a 12-hour journey, so I had a lot to think about while my back was in continuous pain as I was squashed and sitting in an unsettling position.

I kept looking outside the window while my thoughts raced at the same speed as the scenery outside. I noticed our route changed from city life to the countryside. There was a lot of off-roading as well. But it felt nice to look outside for a longer period of time after so long.

Life, death. Justice, injustice, stars, darkness, God, the devil. I had nearly covered all the topics I could think of, but my brain refused to be quiet; I was entering the unknown again.

Finally, at 2 AM in the morning, we reached the prison. What I saw was a mix of beautiful scenic paintings with a touch of disaster. How? Well, the building I stood in front of was nothing like the dungeon I was in earlier. It had trees and bushes surrounded by birds chirping, along with mountains that could be seen from inside the prison as well. It was quite open and spacious, unlike the one I was in before. When I stepped inside, that is when I got ahold of the disaster it was in. It was dirty and overcrowded. I stayed in Arthur Road with 2 other people for most of my time there; all of a sudden, shifting with sixty people in one barrack was something I was no longer used to.

Luckily for me, two friends of mine from prison were also sentenced around the same time, so they came here along with me.

One was a Nigerian guy, who was unfortunately sentenced to 30 years, and the other one was a lad from North India, precisely from Manipur. They were with me in the van as well.

They made us step out of the van in a queue and took our bags to the go-down after they were searched. All the cigarettes and everything else were taken from us; basically, the people from the new jail did a thorough search. After that, we were allocated to the after barrack in the 8 no. area, which had six barracks called 8/1 up to 8/6. The barracks, however, were quite small, and they were overcrowded with dirty toilets. It was like I had come back in time when I had to get water from the well for washing dishes and for the toilet, which was at the back of the barrack with just a hole in the floor and a small door. There was one white and black TV of 19 inches and a couple of fans.

Initially, we met people who were convicted from Arthur Road. They had heard of me there, so they came up and spoke to me. All of us, me, the Nigerian and the Manipur guy, managed to be allocated to the same area, which was in the number 1 circle within two buildings. This circle had four barracks, I was allocated to 1/4, and my friends went to 1/1. So, when the barracks were open, we were all together.

I met one lad during my initial days in Arthur Road who was quite educated. He worked in the money-ordering process for prisoners, so he knew I got money orders every month. He requested me to join his *handi*, mainly because I could contribute to buying extra items from the canteen. I, too, needed to make friends around here, so I joined this *handi.* There were only four of us, but the place was so congested that when everybody rolled out their mats to sleep, there was no floor space visible.

The atmosphere was quite different there, mainly because everyone was convicted. So, the hope was gone; everyone was always a bit down. People were more like ghosts over here. Some had forgotten they had families, and some families had forgotten about them. Nonetheless, I started getting into a routine over the next few weeks, playing ludo and games and exercising every day in hopes of just passing my time. The worst thing at that moment was that the only contact I had with my family members was through letters, which I had to write to Rey, who would then scan and email to everyone at home. So the process was quicker and cheaper than posting directly home.

Over time, the situation got worse. I was getting panic attacks again; it was like I had gone back to day one. I kept thinking I needed to get out. My mum was getting desperate as well. Meanwhile, my mum agreed to give £1,000 to Gawankar to get started on the plan.

It was late September, and it was time to get started on my escape plan. I needed my family to at least come over for a month. When they finally did, they brought my brother's passport with a valid visa inside, my son Kyle brought the passport with him, and a friend outside was arranging to get the visa authorised with an entry stamp as though my brother had entered the country. This was so there would be no problems at the airport for the exit stamp when I hopefully boarded the outbound flight. The plan was to pose as my brother because my brother looked very similar to me and get out of this country. It was just a rough idea initially, then Santosh got me connections, and I was willing to execute it finally.

However, the following few weeks were horrendous; I had no contact and didn't know what was going on outside. I had thoughts about whether the plan would work out or not and whether all the arrangements would be made on time. I had a million thoughts. What worried me the most was that I wasn't in coordination with them, and I knew Kyle had to be in the hospital bed over the next ten days for the police to come and check for verification.

I received a letter in October saying Alf and Kyle were in Mumbai and the work was going on. The following days were pure agony because, with each passing day, I just didn't know what was happening. Again, I was listening to the speaker system every day, praying it would be my name called or for any other bits of news.

In this new prison, there was a library that had a big map of the world on the wall, including a detailed map of India. I used to take every chance I got to go to the library and plan my escape. There was a luxury bus I planned on taking to Delhi and then crossover the border into Nepal to book my flight, a 36-hour journey approximately, and I would be out of the country.

It was a hard time; each day was torture until, after a month, I finally found out my fate. Rey had hired a car and a driver and came to Kolhapur for a visit with Kyle and Alf.

I knew from their faces it was bad news; Rey was crying, and my family were close to tears as well. They told me Kyle had spent 5 days in the hospital while all the relevant paperwork was organised. Gawanker applied for parole before the high court judge, but he rejected it on the grounds of me being a foreigner and a flight risk.

Gawankar didn't give up, though; Kyle went back to JJ Hospital for 5 days while the new paperwork was arranged again, and then he approached the new judge in the high court. This judge granted me 5 days of conditional bail to go and visit Kyle in the hospital. He said I would stay in Arthur Road and be escorted to JJ Hospital from 9 AM and return at 4 PM. Also, I would need ten guards, and I would have to bear the expense, which would be close to £2,000. So, that plan failed as obviously I could not escape with a guard escort.

What is your will against the will of God?

I was devastated, and all my plans and dreams were shattered. I wondered how many more kicks in the teeth I could take before they were all knocked out for good. I felt worse for my family. My poor mum and sister and also my dad in England, along with countless cousins and friends. I felt most for Kyle and Alf right then, though. They looked exhausted. The stress takes a toll, and the harrowing depravity they witnessed in JJ Hospital combined with the travel, well, a little bit of me died that day looking into their eyes. We only got a ten-minute visit, and I had to reluctantly wave them goodbye, wondering when or whether I would ever see them again.

Rey had given the guards money to pass me a few letters in, so I took these back to the barrack. They were off to mum, a few others and a long-awaited one from my girlfriend.

It started off nice enough, what she and her daughter had been doing, going on holiday and general things. There wasn't much content as far as a "*Dear John*" goes. It was something along the lines of: '*There will always be a place in my heart for you, and I've waited all this time, but I've got to think about mine and my daughter's future'.*

I saw it coming anyway, and I understood why as well. I mean, why would someone put their lives on halt for me? She didn't deserve the three and a half years of waiting even. I guess it just wasn't meant to be. Besides, the emptiness in the page spoke more than her words. It was clear there was no way back, and I totally understood it. Even I had bigger problems to handle at my end, so it sort of took over. I made a promise to myself then to block her out and concentrate on what my next move would be.

You lose people, and you move on, but a part of you stays back, reminiscing how things were when they were around.

Chapter Eleven

The anger in you that you are not able to express begins to reflect in your personality.

There's this fire inside you that burns. It burns you and everything else you touch along the way. The worst part is that there's no end to it. When something burns on the outside, it turns to ashes. But when you burn on the inside, you just keep on burning. The rage keeps getting intense, but the irony is that you don't turn into ashes. You're just there, watching it happen, realising there's not much you can do about it.

Over time I became aggressive with people. This was mostly because the place was very crowded, which made me anxious. It was a shock for me to have all these uneducated people around me. I nearly had a few fights and was snapping over the smallest things, especially over water.

After a lot of investigating, it came to light that there were separate cells in the hospital which were meant to be for the sick. There were also a few separate cells in the 6, 7, and 8 no. areas. Since I was on edge and engaging in fights every day, I requested the superintendent to move me to one of the separates before the situation escalated. He was clearly not convinced and even tried to convince me to adjust where I was allocated. But I stood my ground. Soon after, although I preferred a cell in 6, 7, or 8, he agreed to the hospital area, and I was shifted there.

While I was being shifted from there, I looked at everyone with an expression that portrayed me as if I was being freed or let go. It was a win-win situation for me as I knew the place I was shifting to would be less crowded, and most of all, I would have my own toilet.

However, upon my arrival, I realised I had made a mistake. The sight in front of me was horrible. It was as if I had entered a world of horror. I thought the worst I'd see would be just a small crowd of sad and sick people, but what I saw was unbelievable. I was surrounded by people who had one arm, one leg, or cancer in their mouths. I even came across people whose faces or bodies were disfigured because of a certain illness. This time, I just had to adjust. I couldn't just keep on changing my mind and asking the superintendent to act accordingly.

"Compromise brings harmony to both,
happiness to none."

— Amit Kalantri

The whole hospital area consisted of 4 barracks, including 16 separate cells. In the centre, there was an office area where the doctor would sit and where the dispensary was. And then to either side were a few beds for the really sick. The two other barracks were for the old men above 60 and for the mentally ill prisoners.

The separate cells were quite modern, I must say. The floors were made of flat tiles, the paint wasn't too bad on the walls either, and above all, something that I looked forward to the most, it was a quiet place. The patients in there were suffering from Tuberculosis or HIV, so they were segregated. Also, There was a nice walkway around the separate cells. I could clearly do some exercises or yoga. However, the best thing about that place was the availability of water around the clock because that is one of the major issues in India. Moreover, keeping a phone was much easy here as there were few people; thus, hiding your belongings was not difficult. In addition to all these, it was a lot more peaceful as compared to my previous place.

The fellow patients there were much better. Though, there were a lot more wardens and watchmen in there. There was also a dwarf in there, and he was in for rape. Quite ironically, he was the sanest one amongst the others. I had some brilliant conversations with him. By that time, I had started picking up 10 to 20 percent of the Hindi language because, in this jail, people were not educated, and only a few individuals knew any English.

A couple of guards came to see me saying they had a message from Santosh. They told me when Kyle left, he gave Rey £1,000, so I now had money to pay the guards and have things my way as well. But since I was new here and was not personally familiar with anyone, I could barely trust the guards. What I did was that I knew one lad over here whom I could trust a little as we chatted a lot. I asked him to arrange a phone for me, to which he agreed and fixed a price of 21,000 rupees. I asked for an internet-compatible phone, so I could also go on social media. The deal was I would get Rey to deposit money in the lad's bank account. I would get two batteries. When one died, I could give it to him, and he would get it charged again. Anyway, he ended up giving me a Nokia, a small square mobile device with just one battery and no internet. This disappointed me, and I was furious. He had taken £250 from me and given me a phone that didn't even cost £10. I had a bit of an argument with him. I told him this wasn't in the deal. But I really couldn't do anything about it at that moment, so I just took that phone for a few weeks. I kept it inside my pillow. The place wasn't searched much as it only contained sick people in it or the elderly. But soon, the battery ran out. Due to this, I went backwards and forward for a couple of months, asking him to charge the battery and charge the phone. I kept silent for a couple of weeks, but one day I lost it and went to his area. I couldn't stop myself from approaching him and addressing the issue. While I stepped towards him, I promised myself to be calm and find a middle solution for it. And I did. I asked him for a camera phone and some batteries. I gave him everything back, and he agreed to do it. But it was of no use because he didn't do anything. I waited for a couple more weeks, and I realised he was just giving me excuses each time for why he couldn't charge the battery.

Soon after, I lost my cool, and to this date, I don't regret it. I literally threatened him. I was desperate, and he was continuously making a fool out of me. All I wanted was to just stay in contact with my family. As soon as he entered my eye frame, I rushed toward him and pushed him. I was clearly furious, and by that time, he was sure of it as well. I told him to give me my phone and a charged battery back as well. Quite honestly, he didn't utter a word. He listened, and even though I was expecting him to disappoint me this time as well but he didn't. He did exactly what I asked him to. He even gave me a charger so I could charge the battery myself somehow.

It is astonishing how people respond better to acts of violence, more than acts of love.

Surprisingly what I was expecting at the back of my head happened. I got a search a week later!

It was clear that the officers had been tipped off that I had a phone on me. Otherwise, they do not usually come into this side of the prison. That too at such odd hours. Normally the search takes place before the count, but these officers barged in after the count when all the prisoners were locked up. I was sure this couldn't have been a coincidence. When I realised a search was ongoing, I quickly hid the phone in my shorts because I had less time and I had it in my hand at that moment.

Luckily, or call it god's plan, they didn't pat me down. They just searched the pillows and trashed the area and realised I had nothing hidden. As soon as I realised I was spared, I told them I'd approach the embassy and make sure the world knows they're specifically treating me like this, to which they responded they had a report against me. That is where my doubt was confirmed. I knew it was the same lad, and he did that for revenge as I had threatened him.

Anyway, I carried on with my days there. I started pinpointing all the positive things I saw in front of me. I had my own toilet and space, and it was quiet. I mean, I just had more privacy there. Meanwhile, I texted Taraq Sayed. He said he would request the judge for a time frame for the appeal to start. He told me he was going to file an expedition order. He was basically looking to expedite the case.

The days just passed by. They would have gone by even if I had stopped breathing.

The world doesn't stop for anyone or anything you see. But you do. You do put your life on halt; for something, for someone.

What is the first thought on your mind when you look at the sky? Because that is what means the most to you.

Chapter Twelve

The years I spent inside the prison taught me things I wouldn't have learned otherwise. It is said the wisest are the ones with the most wounds. Wisdom cannot be apprehended by just anyone out there. The path to it requires courage and the will to absorb pain-like knowledge. And that is what I exactly did.

Five years with people of different colours, ages, and religions, made my personality flexible. This series of unfortunate events led me to a state that was adaptive, predictive, and compromising. By now, I could understand a bit of their language too. There wasn't any need for a translator or a middleman anymore. I was on my own, and I was used to it.

"I'd watched too many schoolmates graduate into mental institutions, into group homes and jails, and I knew that locking people up was paranormal - against normal, not beside it. Locks didn't cure; they strangled."

— Scott Westerfeld

I made my routine busy to avoid any sort of depression. I decided to acquire a healthy routine. With the help of a new friend I made, Sanjay, we made weights out of clay. Every morning, we did a little bit of weight training. Sanjay and I turned out to be great friends; the lad was in for murder, and he was in for life. Sometimes, I felt bad for him. He was poor, so he couldn't really buy the basic essentials for himself. I used to get them for him. He was in the cell next to me with two other men. We used to get the food by four or 4:40 PM, so it was mostly served cold. The best thing that came out of our friendship was that I used to give him all the ingredients, like the masala and peanut butter, etc., and he used to make innovative recipes out of it. The food he made was hot, and he put the *daal* or the *bhajiya* in a small plastic bag and tied it with a string. This was after the count, and the whistle was blown. Everybody was locked up by then. There was a two-meter gap between each cell gate. After he had tied the food, I used to throw a piece of weighted string all the way across, with the help of which he used to tie the weighted string to the small bags. I used to pull my hot food through it and eat it. We used to play a lot of ludo as well, along with a lot of other games, anything to pass the time, basically. We got by very well as he spoke a little bit of English, and I had picked up 10 percent of Hindi by then.

It was winter, probably the month of November or December. The nights were quite cold. I contacted my mum and asked her to send me a white jumper or a coat, and a white bubble hat and some gloves. This is because, at the prison, you were only allowed to wear white, regardless of what it was.

Christmas came again. In this prison, whenever an occasion was around the corner, especially Christmas and Easter, we were allowed to buy chicken and *paneer*. Paneer is like little cubes of cheese. So the prison that had almost 1500 people, you can imagine them making 3000+ KG of that stuff.

Whenever the Christmas period kicks in, we're allowed to buy all of that with our money. I remember buying a sponge cake from a bakery within the prison. People used to come and work there. At the backhand of the prison, there was a woodwork area, a welding area, along with a bunch of farmers. Some of the prisoners worked as farmers to get all the vegetables. There was washing, ironing, and a lot of other services. Several people worked there as there were many buildings for different purposes. The bakery used to make pastries and different sweet items that you could also buy from the canteen with the PPC money.

Around Christmas time, they also made these sponge cakes which were for around 100 rupees. We bought six of them and made it a little bit easier for everyone around us. I mean, it was an occasion, so we did a little extra. Everyone at the prison wished each other a Merry Christmas, whether it was a Hindu, a Muslim, or someone from any other religion. We always respected each other's religion.

In the next few months of 2014, up until May, I was having trouble charging my Nokia phone. As I mentioned, I had a charger, but since there was no electricity inside the cell, not even a fan or a radio, it was of no use as there was really no place to connect a charger.

There was a TV in the barrack, and I could connect my phone there, but unfortunately, there were a lot of informants in the area; hence it was impossible to charge your phone on the TV without being caught or informed. But the good thing was that within the hospital area, at the back, there was a small shed with a lot of electronics in there.

I also had a friend there who was a doctor. Well, he was a doctor when he was outside, but he was convicted of rape. He was also quite westernised. I used to train with him alongside Sanjay. He was called Vanee.

Vanee was in for life, but he was a fully qualified doctor, so he used to work alongside the doctors in the dispensary, also checking everyone's blood pressure and giving injections. He had obviously gained a lot of trust in all these years as he was given a key to a building that was behind the hospital barrack within our area. So I used to get in this place a few times, I got a razor, but I managed to get a blade, scraped a wire, and tried to hook my charger.

The following two or three weeks, whenever I noticed I had time to go there and connect my phone, whether it was for 5 minutes, I did. But unfortunately, it did not work. As I was in a situation those days, I was really desperate to get my phone charged.

When I arrived at the jail, there was a friend from Arthur Road that I used to be with, in 1 number circle. His name was Emile Jerome Mathew, and he was a Navy officer, but he was in for the murder of his girlfriend's lover.

The story goes like once, the guy flew back from Kochi to Mumbai unannounced and found his girlfriend with her lover in a compromising position, or so he said. They killed him together, but according to what I've heard, he stabbed him and chopped his body into three hundred pieces and hid the body somewhere. Maria Susairaj was his girlfriend's name, and she was equally involved in the murder. It was clearly a *crime of passion*. However, we used to get along really well as he was quite westernised. I was with him from January 2010 in 1 number barrack until December 2010 in the Anda Barrack. He was also in my area.

But unfortunately, he took a severe beating from the officers in 2009, after which he filed a complaint in the High court. Clearly, there was friction between him and the officers. One morning, they took him out, and I never heard from him again. Although I did hear something along the lines that he was convicted for ten years for destroying evidence and shifted to Kaulapur, and his girlfriend was given three years.

Moving on, when I came to Kaulapur, I asked around for him, but at that time, he was out on parole. When he came back, I had moved to the hospital area. Emile was quite intelligent. He used to work on the computers in the office area and on the computers within the library area. As he was in the clerical work in the prison, he was free to go where ever he pleased without the warden or watchmen's permission.

He used to visit me two to three times a week, and it was actually good meeting him as he used to update me about the latest news and television series, such as Game of Thrones and new music. Basically, he used to keep me up to date regarding the current world and affairs.

Anyway, since I was in desperate need of a phone, he told me there was a Samsung up for sale. He arranged the deal between me and somebody else, and I passed the Nokia and gave 5000 rupees extra by transferring it into his account. The deal was that when he received the money and the Nokia phone, he would then pass me the Samsung along with two fully charged batteries.

Finally, for the next few months, I was again in contact with my family. I used to sit on the floor with my back against the wall and act like I was reading a newspaper or a book and keeping an eye out for the guards or informants, while I actually used to send texts to my family and a few friends. I never called because I really couldn't risk it. You never could tell when the guards were going to turn up.

Also, I arranged to get myself some money; Kyle left me over £1,000 with Ray. I arranged a deal with a guard and gave him a commission, and got myself 4000 in cash. I then contacted my mum and asked her to send me some reading material, word searches, and magazines. When that arrived, my two-star officer rejected it because some of the magazines had bikini models in them. The environment there wasn't very liberal. Any sort of naked flesh wasn't allowed. So then I gave him 1000 rupees, and I finally got them posted.

In the hospital area, patients with tuberculosis and HIV were given two boiled eggs per day. So I spoke with a three-star officer who often asked me for money. This time, I told him that I wouldn't give him money for free and arranged for myself two boiled eggs every day as well.

However, I got one boiled egg every day, and it was still something good to mix with the food.

In around February, I got another search! This was a morning search. Much before we opened at 5:30 AM, I had hidden my phone in the pillow. Basically, the pillows in prison were filled with the hair of the coconut. However, they tossed everything around and couldn't really find it. I continued to use that Samsung for the next few months.

If I go back again, in mid-2012, when I was in Arthur Road, I was having really bad knee pain. Now one of the therapists in there, he was actually a qualified physiotherapist. He used to come and treat me every morning. The pain was so severe that I was limping. He used to come and help me stretch and tell me what to do. I was wearing a kneecap. And that is exactly what I was using to bring the batteries and the pen drive for the TV in from the court.

In January 2014, embassy personnel visited me. I told them I had this pain and I needed an MRI scan. The problem was that Kaulapur did not facilitate government hospitals, so it would mean that I had to be transferred back to Arthur Road, and frankly, that was what I exactly wanted.

I then placed an application, which was a long process. The application went to the DIG, which stands for Director Inspector General. They run all the prisons in Western Maharashtra. However, nothing happened.

The embassy personnel visited me every three months, and I kept telling them that there was no progress. Luckily at this point, Nawaz, who was a member of the embassy, used to come and visit me all the time. She had a direct number for the DIG. Long story short, she arranged with the DIG and made sure I got guards.

Around 9:30 AM on May 12 or, maybe, 15, I remember it was after my birthday, I was busy doing my exercise when I got a call to the office. I went to the senior superintendent. He said, "Alright, get your stuff. You're going to Pune."

When you're in the middle of nowhere, you tend not to give up. Your life is like a game of dominos, fragile and delicate. You carefully walk through it, and as soon as you gain momentum, someone knocks it all down, and there, that very moment, you lose.

Chapter Thirteen

You hit rock bottom and think about what could be worse until the ground breaks and you realise there's more.

I looked at him in disbelief and said, "What?"

He said it again in a stern voice, "Go get your stuff. The van is waiting. You're going to Pune to Sassoon General Hospital, and you'll be allocated to Yerawada Central Prison."

I was shocked. All I wanted was to go somewhere known, not back into the unknown again! This would be the third prison I was being transferred to. I was certainly not ready to start it all over again.

"You could at least give me a week's notice. I have my stuff to pack and things to do. I had to shower as well. And why Sassoon General Hospital in Pune? I could just go to the JJ Hospital and get my MRI there."

The superintendent was annoyed, maybe because I kept insisting for more than five minutes.

"No. It's decided. Pune is just 5 hours away. Hence, it's closer. Just get your work done, and once you're over with it, you can come back here," said the superintendent.

The thing I was worried about the most was the phone. I was going to a new place, and I had just been here for six or seven months. Sanjay was the only close friend I had here, so I rushed toward him to seek help. Unfortunately, there was a yoga session going on. A few yoga trainers had come for classes, and Sanjay was inside. I remember that I was panicking. However, I somehow managed to get him out of the session to the side and said, "Look, I need your help. I've got this phone and you..." to which he gave me a look and interrupted, "Kala Topi! Kala Topi!" Kala basically means black in Hindi, and Topi means cap. Gandhi always wore a white cap. So what he meant by Kala Topi was that I was really clever and smart. He wasn't angry, rather just surprised that he didn't know about it either. As I mentioned, Sanjay was a good friend. He comforted me and said he'd take care of it.

"Don't worry, mate. I'll dig and hide it in the ground somewhere. Leave that to me."

As soon as I handed him the phone, I went and took a shower. I took a few belongings with me and, of course, left a few with Sanjay. I didn't actually take the belongings with me. When you're a prisoner, you have to deposit your stuff into the godown, and then it is transferred to your next jail. The stuff I decided to take with me had three bags of clothes and a lot of essentials like toothpaste, soups, and ariel packets for washing the clothes. I brought two buckets with me as well. I actually got in the van outside, and the guards took me to the Kaulapur bus station. All this time, they kept me handcuffed. I told them I wouldn't run. At least release me. I mean, it was bad enough to be escorted by guards. I didn't want to be too embarrassed, you know. I could feel the stares all over me. It really wasn't a nice feeling.

Anyway, we eventually boarded the bus to Pune, Yerawada Jail. It was a continuous 5-hour journey. When we were halfway through, they took my handcuffs off. I thought to myself, *it really didn't matter inside the bus. It was outside that affected me.*

Moving on, they handcuffed me again before getting off the bus to our destination.

The DIG of Western Maharashtra had her office in the jail, so the police were extra strict and careful there. All they wanted was the best in this situation.

Just to explain how strict the jail was: they squeezed my toothpaste out to see if I had hidden anything in there. I mean, how can I put something inside toothpaste? They checked my items, unboxed my cigarettes, undressed me, and even checked my underwear. It was awkward. After the search, they took me to the After Barrack.

It was a massive jail when I first walked in. There were around four thousand prisoners. Even though it is a city jail, there were a lot of trees and birds in there. The second I entered, I was surprised by how spacious it was, unlike Mumbai. There was a lot of open air. I had a ten-minute walk at the back of the prison while going to the After Barrack. The After Barrack was the same as the previous ones, just darker, dirtier, and damper. It was horrendous. There was nothing on the walls. In jails and other barracks, people had their belongings with them as they lived there, but the After Barrack was somewhat of a waiting area for prisoners.

There were probably eighty people or so around that night. I spent my time speaking to different people when the food came in. Like before, I couldn't make hot food in there. It was really strict. They gave us tin plates which were heated and covered in black. The warden poured in daal, and it was actually leaking. I had no spoon and really had no idea how to eat it. It was just horrible to think I'd gone back to this situation. It was like I had progressed, and things were going my way in the other prison. But then, all of a sudden, I was back to square one.

As soon as the sleeping time came, they gave us one mat. The area was huge, and approximately a hundred could sleep over there. But they made us lie down like sardines in a quarter of a barrack, and the rest was left as an empty space. I still don't understand why. The prisoner that was in charge at that time was quite arrogant. He was roaming around, hitting people with a stick. I really couldn't stand it and wanted to get this over with, to get done with my MRI and return to Kaulapur to my phone, most importantly.

The next day, a three-star officer came down to me, and he was actually an officer at Arthur Road, so he recognised me. He told me he was transferred to Pune in 2010.

Sunday came, and I had to shower, but I didn't have my clothes and my towel as they had not yet released my items from the godown. I spent my Sunday just walking here and there, wishing time to just pass on quickly. There were no games or any sort of activity in there. Everyone was rowdy, as I observed. I got food, and then it was the same thing at night. We actually went down, and they were writing everyone's names. Everyone was sitting in a queue, but I put my legs out because of my knee. I couldn't fit and fold my legs like that.

There were prisoners talking in Marathi (the language of Maharashtra), and a lot of them were asking me questions, two of them in particular. I couldn't understand it as it was a bit different from Hindi. But I could understand a little bit by the aggression of their tone that they were pricks, basically. They had these sticks, and they were hitting people. And they used to find out who was in for what crime and then bully them accordingly. They were spotting people out of the crowd and then scaring them. Soon, they saw me.

"Hey, you! What's your name?"

"Barry, Barry Hulse."

"Cross your legs!" And they put the stick on my legs to scare me.

I was furious. This behaviour was totally unacceptable. I looked at him in anger and said, "If that stick touches my leg again, I'll beat your ass with it!"

We had a bit of a stand-off. I then told him I had a knee problem in Hindi, so he finally understood. Clearly, he didn't understand English. However, he disliked me, and I didn't like him either, as he was arrogant and bossy. We also had a bit of a fun night on a Sunday as he tried to force me to sleep like the rest as well, but I stayed put. I told him I was not an

Indian. I was not like these people. Why should I sleep like this? I have been in prison for four years. I am not an idiot.

The next morning, I went to the super intendant and asked him to get me moved the same day. But unfortunately, he told me it could not happen until Tuesday. So I requested him to at least get me my own *bistar* – bed in Hindi. I finally collected my stuff and the bedding, which included the *kumbal* as well, from the godown and had a long-awaited shower. In the barrack, besides the warden, no one else had their own bedding but me. I had to tell and convince the warden beforehand to avoid any inconveniences. I had a good night's sleep on a Monday.

Tuesday morning, they called me before breakfast to go for check-in. We went into this room, and there were around twelve of us, and they always say Jodi, Jodi – a couple in Hindi, and everyone jumps into pairs. It makes them easier to count, I suppose.

The check-in consisted of taking pictures and filling out forms on a computer. Everybody sat down and folded their legs, so I asked them if I could sit on the bench as I had a knee problem.

"Oh, special foreigner, eh?" But he agreed and said I could sit on the bench.

There was this old guy and a younger lad. The people were asking what they were in for and if it was rape. As they exchanged words, I kept listening and observing. As soon as he released his details, I wished I had never heard it in the first place. It was the rape of a six-year-old. He tempted her over the chocolate and took her in somehow, and raped the girl. It was sickening. It is the worst crime in mankind; to torture a child like that. I was also sickened by the prisoners' reaction. I really couldn't understand why everyone was laughing.

Tuesday night, they allocated me to a new area. They told me I'd be going to the 1-number circle. In the Yerawada Jail, the convicted prisoners go to 1 number circle or 3 number circle. In between is two number circle, also known as the After Barrack, where I was initially.

There was a total of 8 barracks, and one and three were the same. It's a huge area, and it's sort of circular. In the centre, there's a watch tower. Each barrack has a big gate attached to it, along with a factory of sewing machines. Every barrack can hold hundred people with just one washroom. They have a common toilet in the outside area and a small walkway for the prisoners to go and shower, which is like a well on the turf. The toilet was similar to the previous toilets.

Moving on, I met someone who was my in-charge in Arthur Road for about three years. He was really close to me, like a good friend. The moment he saw me, he ran toward me, asking what had happened. Obviously, he didn't expect me there. Hence, I told him what happened, and we spoke a little about the people on Arthur Road. I asked him if he could place me in the 8-number barrack with a Nigerian I had met earlier. He said he would look into it. However, he put me in the 5-number barrack of 1 number circle.

When I entered my new area, I saw a few friendly faces. As I was a foreigner, everybody was interested in knowing why I was sentenced and where I was from. I joined the *handi.* There was a big guy in there, kind of like a bodybuilder. His name was Nitin. It was his *handi,* and he had a worker with him to bring the food and clean, etc.

The barrack was quite long. There were ninety people in there. There was a 3-foot place on the side, and there was a walkway in the centre. Surprisingly, the place was very well-cleaned and lit. The paint on the walls was nice as well.

There was a guy named Narender Bhai in there. Everyone called him Bhai, as he was a gangster from Pune. He was in the same barrack as me. Maybe that is why out of all the eight barracks, number five was the best maintained.

There were around fifteen to twenty toilets around, maybe. There were some rules made by Narender bhai, not by the prison, some of which were to clean the toilets every day. I was only allowed to use the toilets that were outside.

In the corner, there was a little exercise area where we had weights of all ranges and benches made of stone for bench presses. And there was a pull-up bar. Moreover, it had a badminton place with a net in the factory area as well. It was absolutely fantastic to have all of that as time passed.

We got into a routine. I used to exercise with Nitin, the bodybuilder from the handi group. He was really good at it, so I used to weight-train every morning with him and a few others.

A week passed by, and I went to the superintendent. I told him I needed guards as I had been brought here to go to Sassoon General Hospital for an MRI. A week had gone by, but nothing happened.

It wasn't all bad, though. The world cup was going on, so I used to watch it on TV and pass my time. I was also in contact with a girl from home, and she was writing me letters that cheered me up every single time. (In a world of instant messaging, value the people who write you letters.)

When you're a foreigner and in an Indian jail, you're a prize for all the locals. They look at you with grave curiosity and question you about things so basic, so elementary. For example, they'd ask you how many times you had sex or if you have ever lived with a woman who's not your wife. For them, it's one life and one wife. Mostly, the questions revolved around women and romance, but there were a few different ones too.

Chapter Fourteen

You think you've got a grip on life, but that's where you're wrong. Your life is like a heartbeat. It's constantly moving and unsteady. The only time you think you're about to get a grip on it is right before you lose it all.

I had been in Yerawada for three weeks, and my three-monthly visits were due from Navaz, who worked for the British Embassy. I had already previously sent a "shopping list" over by post for my essential items, and she brought the usual vitamins/ jam and body lotions, etc. As I mentioned, the prison was really strict and refused me all the items. The embassy's point was that if this is allowed in one jail, it should be allowed everywhere. Besides, a couple of essential items wouldn't harm anyone either. Regardless of how concerned they were, their request was refused. After arguing with the senior Superintendent, I managed to get about 70% of my items. The British Embassy then decided to highlight the main issue. I was brought here to go to Sassoon hospital, and three weeks had passed by, but I still had no guard escort.

So finally, a few days later, on a Saturday, I got guards. I went to Sassoon Hospital, and the sight was unbelievable. I saw dead bodies being pushed around outside the building and all types of horrifying sights. I remember I stood next to a bin in there, and there was a woman of about 85 years old who was chewing "Paan" or "Gutka," which is a prepared betel leaf used as a stimulant, but all it really does is make their mouths red. The worst thing about it is that it is splattered everywhere as people spit it on the walls, floor, and almost everywhere. So I was looking here and there, analysing the hospital and its surroundings, when I heard a sudden, loud and horrible sound of someone clearing their throat. My reflexes responded immediately, and I stepped back and looked. The old lady had spit the "Gutka" out of her mouth, thankfully in the bin, and was wiping her red mouth after it. Quite honestly, it was the most disgusting thing to watch. I rolled my eyes and thought to myself, where am I? I felt like I had gone back a thousand years.

Moving on, we went in and met the doctor. Obviously, I was still with the guards and in handcuffs. I informed him about my situation. The quicker I wanted this to end, the more delayed it got. The doctor told me my MRI could not be done right now. Instead, they could book me in with a sixteen days gap. I took a deep breath and told myself what else can I do anyway. I went back and continued my routine. I somehow managed to get by those slow and depressing sixteen days, and finally, the day to get my MRI done arrived.

As if I wasn't mentally tortured enough, the guards didn't show up. I went to my superintendent and said, "Look, I was supposed to go to Sassoon today for my MRI scan, but the guards haven't shown up. If I miss it today, I will have to go in and book another appointment with a sixteen days gap again."

I was really frustrated, it had been over six weeks there, and I couldn't take it anymore. It was late June, and there was still no rain, so there was an excessive water problem. Some mornings there wasn't even enough for toilet use or showering. With each passing day, I was growing frustrated. The biggest stress at that moment was not being able to contact my family. The superintendent assured me it wouldn't take this long this time and tried his best to calm me down. My frustration was quite visible on my face and my expressions. I didn't even know if my family was okay or not. Most importantly, they didn't know about me either. I kept telling the superintendent that I wanted to go back to Kolhapur as I did not want to stay there for months. He tried his best to assure me it wouldn't be months, but I stood my ground. I told him I wanted to go back, and that's it.

Finally, about four to five days later, they told me to get myself ready as I was going back. I said goodbye to everyone I knew and spent time with. Clearly, a lot of them weren't quite happy to see me go as they had fun asking me questions regarding western culture, and I had made a few good friends. It was a Saturday, and they handcuffed me again and put me in the van as we first had to go to the bus station. After the tiring route on two buses and carrying my belongings in two plastic bags, we arrived back at the Kolhapur Prison around maybe 8 PM. After being searched and all my administration work completed, I was placed in the after barrack. The next day was a Sunday, so I wasn't moved back to my area. I was just wondering and worrying whether I would get my cell phone back again as I was gone for longer than I had planned. On Monday, when I was moved back to my old separate area, I took my phone from Sanjay as if I was starving and had seen food after days. I realised it was not charged. Unfortunately, the battery had died. I was a bit devastated. I was again in the same position for which I had to fight before; a cellphone with no batteries charged. I held it together. I kept focusing on the bright side; let's just say that in Yerawada, I was locked up for 19 hours, my barrack had 105 or more people in, and again it was so dull, damp, and dirty that I really wanted to go back to Kohlapur. I couldn't stand it here.

Over the next couple of months, I got back to exercising for two hours in the mornings and got into a general routine. I used to walk in the afternoons for fifty minutes or so with a dwarf called Sandip. He was serving a seven years sentence for rape. I always wondered how he had the strength to miscreant a full-grown woman. He couldn't speak English but was probably the most intelligent prisoner in the hospital area, and with my improved Hindi, we had some good conversations.

In 2005, I was in Goa with my son Kyle, my mum, and my better half, and we were on the beach. In India, the men hold hands casually as they walk. It's as natural as us English slapping backs or shaking hands. Over the first hour, four or five Indian lads who were friends had walked by, fingers locked and swinging arms, when mum said, "Baz, is this area of the beach for gay people?" It is bizarre to behold when you are from a completely different culture, and I thought the same on my first vacation here in 2001. So basically, from day one in prison, while walking with prisoners, they would casually grab my hands! I always explained that in my culture, it seemed like an affectionate gesture and only done with your partner. I didn't mind with Sandip, though, as I would imagine it was Kai, my grandson, when I held his tiny hands, and we walked and chatted.

The jail was quite free at that time. However, if any incident occurred, it became really strict. In the year 2013, a prisoner called Davendra Jagtat (DJ) got a country-made revolver into Taloja jail in Mumbai on the way back from court. He fired at Abu Salem, an accused of the 1993 bomb blast. He was expatriated from Portugal along with his actress girlfriend Monica Bedi in 2002. Salem and Dossa had problems in Arthur Road with each other, and Dossa slashed Salem's face. Mustafa Dossa had ordered the shooting at Taloja jail for revenge. DJ was Santosh's old gang member as a shooter. Santosh had been meeting Mustafa inside the prison a lot, so the media had said that the two of them had organised it. Therefore we had no phone or other privileges for weeks as outside police searches kept coming. It actually helped Salem's case, though, as the Portuguese government only deported him with the guarantee of his safety and no death sentence. Obviously, his safety had been compromised.

So Kolhapur was on lockdown at this time as some idiot had filmed inside Anda Barrack, cooking and smoking ganja, and managed to get the sim card out to the tv and media. So this meant I had no chance to charge my phone's batteries now, and the searches were too frequent to change anything, so I had to leave it on the ground. I still hear the screams of the eight lads who made the video at 6 AM. They were dragged out and beaten to a pulp under the watchful eye and orders of the DIG.

Note to self; never humiliate the authorities.

One morning, Sanjay got into an argument with some watchman. This guy had abused him in Hindi, so Sanjay got him to the ground and hit him. I and some other friends of Sanjay kept saying Sanjay wasn't wrong. He was provoked, and the other guy had started it. Around 11 o'clock, we all got called to the superintendent's office. The superintendent came to the conclusion that we all should be sent to different barracks. I wasn't ready for this, obviously. My phone was on the ground at the back of the cell.

At 11:30 AM, at a lock-in, the circle officer came and told everybody to get their belongings together. He came to me and said, "You'll be going in a different barrack now," but I stayed put.

I said, "I want a separate cell and want to talk to the embassy." I gave it a thought and then requested the different barrack to be in 6 no. circle because Enile was in there. Another reason was that I had been there before and saw how relaxed it was there. There were only around eighty people in there, most of which were workers. This meant it would be empty most of the time as the people would be working. It was a premeditated decision, to be honest. The area was quite spacious as well, and the vibes were better than what we got in the other barracks. It was a bit older looking and dirtier than the hospital area because six, seven, and eight no. circles contained separate cells built in the 19th century, but that is what I wanted, so I was okay with it. Before they asked me to shift, I requested time to pack my belongings, which included my cell phone. However, they refused and said I had to go right now. It surely wasn't like I had much of a choice. I was allocated to the new area—6 no. circle.

New beginnings are supposed to bring new joys and new adventures, whereas new beginnings in my life meant new torments and new tragedies. Hope is tricky. It keeps you going with an assumed promise of a happy ending. I dreaded if I was to end like Hachiko, the dog who waited for his master for ten years and then took his last breath.

Chapter Fifteen

When you are ready to give up, you find new hope, a shining ray of light that keeps you moving, but when that only ray of light is taken away, the only thing you are left with is complete hollowness, disappointment, and hopelessness.

It was October 2014, nearly five years now, being in India in three different prisons, and I was moving again! I was settled in the hospital's separate area; the cells were fifty metres from the nearest barracks where the other prisoners were kept, and it was quiet at night. They were all either over seventy or had mental health problems. It was sad, but it also helped to pass the days watching their daily crazy and hysterical antics. It was also good for meeting others there who had come to see the doctor or to collect medications.

The separate cells were in two blocks, facing each other, and my mobile was underneath the ground at the back of my cell. The prisoners in the separate cells had skin problems, HIV, TB (Tuberculosis), etc. So, when I was asked to move out and change the area, I obviously needed my mobile phone with me. The in charge of that area came around and asked me to move out. I asked for some time to get my belongings together, specifically after 3 pm, so I could get out and pick up the phone to take to the new area with me.

However, unfortunately, one of the persons in charge came and said, "There is no time to pack up your belongings now". He ordered everybody to move out.

We were all sent out to the Mandel Karia, which is like a small hut where the jailer (two-star officer) sits. They tried to allocate me back to one of the barracks. It was indeed something that I should be stressing about, as I was a foreigner who was unaware of their culture and language. Being a foreign national, it was difficult for me to get adapted to so many people instantly. I needed my own space. I told them I could not speak the same language, so it would be stressful for me to live with so many people in this area. He agreed with me and put me in 6 no. circle. I was glad as my old friend back from 2010 was actually in that area as well. It was a relief to know a familiar and friendly face would be there to help me get through difficult times. They agreed to my terms as they were getting paid for this at that time. I provided them with some cash, which was enough to have them convinced. They agreed that I should stay separate, and I was moved to 6 no. circle.

Every circle in prison has barracks, and the 6 no. circle has two small ones. Each had the capacity for approximately forty to sixty people. I was allocated number twenty-five. The cell numbers started going up from twenty-one to thirty-five. From this place, I was able to see the entry gate at the boundary wall. The kitchen staff prisoners slept in the 1 no. barrack of the 6 no. circle. They do two shifts there, night and day. When the night shift people used to be working, the day shift people were sleeping, and vice versa. To be honest about it, the sleeping cycle created a peaceful atmosphere in the 6 no. circle.

In the 2 no. barrack of the 6 no. circle, there were around twenty-five to thirty lads, and only four or five separate cells were occupied. For this very reason, I wanted 6 no. circle as it was less occupied compared to everywhere else in prison.

When I arrived at the 6 no. circle in 2014, Emile was actually on parole. You can file for parole or furlough after conviction, and at that time, it was twelve-week and four weeks, respectively. Emile was very bright, and he used to take advantage of this by providing all necessary paperwork and going home approximately twice a year. You need valid reasons, e.g. death of a close relative, illness, etc., but in India, for most things, you can pay for the police/doctor reports. The circle consisted of two barracks with a block of 15 separate cells, a run of around ten outside toilets, and the mandatory rectangular well-type of structure where the barrack's prisoners could wash.

Over the next few weeks, I was still facing the same problem of getting my mobile phone from the hospital area. Regrettably, at that time within the prison, you can say that it was a difficult period. The strictness was too much, and it was one of the challenges that I had to face during my time in prison. Any incident could occur within the premises of the prison or within the walls of other jails in Maharashtra, and you would have to be alert for any possibility, especially when you are unable to get in contact with anyone. The security was extraordinarily gruelling and sturdy, but still, they were incompetent in carrying out proper searches. Someone had been slashed over his face and body, and life was tough. The strictness of the prisons can only be imagined; I faced it, and it was soul-destroying.

Since prisoners were not allowed to walk freely anywhere, there had to be an escort to walk along with them. Let's say if anyone needs to go to the library area or the hospital area, they are escorted by either a warden or a watchman.

Convicted prisoners all have to wear a uniform, which consists of a plain, coarse cotton white top, trousers, and a cap/*topi.* The watchman had a blue striped *topi,* and the wardens had a yellow striped *topi* with yellow trousers. So, it was a strict situation for the following five to six weeks. Every chance I got, I would request the circle officer take me to the hospital for some imagined ailment. I would then have to sneak into a separate area to pick up the phone, but each time either the watchman escort was no good, or there were just too many people around. Eventually, with the help of Sanjay keeping watch, I managed to dig it up only to find the hole full of rocks a foot down! I was back to square one with no phone.

Human misery has no boundaries. It's infinite. It defies all laws of nature and does not abide by the rules of society. It is the only thing in the whole wide world that challenges the existence of entropy and completely disregards it.

Rey, my Filipino friend, who was living in Mumbai, was my only flicker of hope. I was thankful that he was keeping me posted with all letters from home. I used to get the embassy to bring me roughly £5,000 worth of postage stamps on each of their visits. Each letter I would send to Rey cost around forty pence for speed post. So, I would send all my letters to Rey, who would then scan them and send them over to mum. She would then print the letters and send them to all my family, friends, and well-wishers. It was the same for replies; when mum collected everyone's letters over the following weeks, she would then send them to Rey via the same procedure, who would print them and send them to me. When sent by speed post, I would receive the letters within three to five days.

In the meantime, over that period, I talked to a number of people in there, and there were a few decent lads. It was different for many people to see me there, as I belong to a western world and not one of the Indians. A foreigner, you could say. So, they liked to talk about western culture and everything. I used to spend hours talking to them sometimes, and they listened to me with great interest. They talked about me most of the time and about my home. How was it possible for me to become a grandfather without marriage, and how did it feel to live in a country that was liberal and free etc. Emile returned from parole, and we got into a routine of walking and exercising in the mornings. He would work in the library and the office from 9:30 am on the computers, but having him there to talk to was what I really needed. An intelligent, western-educated man, he would come back and tell me about all the latest series like GOT and any other English news; he was just someone to whom I could relate, talk about films and music, and somebody who could understand me. It really was a blessing.

Other than Emile, there was another prisoner that I met in my circle, and his name was Javid. He was on a life sentence but also had a pending case, and for this reason, he was getting a court date every fourteen days. Javid had a mobile, and as there are many informers in conviction jails, he asked if he could use it in my cell for ten minutes here and there each day. Obviously, if the officers found out, I could lose my separate cell, so I was very sceptical. I agreed eventually, as long as he would leave it with me on a Sunday so I could contact my people. So, towards the end of 2014, I was content that I had contact and my own space.

The 6 no. separates were approximately 6ft by 10ft, there was a 2ft high wall with a hole in the floor behind, and this was your "privacy". I placed a length of string 6ft high in front of the wall and hung sheets or towels to act as a screen. This way, I could have a wash naked over the whole body without people seeing me.

So basically, I walked outside the cell and watched while he used the phone behind the towels, and I would alert him if any guards were around. I got the phone on Sundays in the deal, as we could only use it in the mornings throughout the week. England is five and a half hours behind India, so it was not viable for me as it was too early at home to call. So, as Sundays were an early lock-in, 11 am to 1 pm, then closed again from 2 pm after collecting the food, there was less staff, and the probability of getting a search in the afternoon or Monday morning was relatively low. Hence, Sunday was ideal for me. My family/ friends were off work, and all of them were available, so I would sit with my back on the wall with a newspaper open on my lap and used to send text messages. My left eye would be on the gate looking for guards, and my right eye would be on the phone under the newspaper. It wasn't worth speaking and risking being caught, so I used to get Rey to top up the credit, and text messages would cost five pence each. I was in contact with most people at home, and on occasions, Emile used to cook me *paneer* from the milk and throw a string from his cell's door to mine, and I would "fish" in the string, which was tied to a bag containing 'hot food", and we used the same operation with the mobile just so he could use it as well. It was good to have Emile as my neighbour, as we could stand at our gate, talk, and joke, and it really helped in spending those seventeen hours locked in.

Out of all the promises about the afterlife, I like the one with a place where there is no suffering. I would like to believe that there is a better place all scarred souls go to after all the horrible things they were subjected to in this world.

Chapter Sixteen

You know evil exists, but you tell yourself otherwise. Regardless of your experiences, you expect. You expect because you give, you expect because you care, and you expect to be treated as you would treat other people. The world, however, doesn't work that way!

So, 2014 came and went, and it was always a little harder for me over Christmas, but the chicken and cake eased the pain a little. In mid-January 2015, Javed, who I had mentioned earlier, had a court date for murder. As I said, I had built a good rapport with him with the phone agreement, and I would jog with him around the barrack in the mornings. As Kolhapur jail was a prison for convicted prisoners, nobody was attending court, which meant it was very difficult to get any items in. Javed was already serving a life sentence but had a second case for robbery and was due in court. Another prisoner and I arranged for money to be transferred to his friend's bank account, and they would then give him the money at court to bring back. I told Rey to transfer around Rs. 6000 (Approximately £50), so I had some cash inside for what I needed.

The Saturday court date came, and Javed got the guards to attend. Normally prisoners would be back within a couple of hours, but as the day went by, he still had not returned. We all came to know at closing time that he had escaped. Three of his friends had arrived at court and had thrown chilli powder into the guard's eyes so he could run. I realised at that point why he would run for two hours every morning. I was happy for him, really, as he was only in his 20s, but my money obviously escaped with him. In India, 99% of the population seemed to be cheaters and dishonest, though. Another similar incident occurred in 2012; my mum got hold of a priest based in Mumbai who promised to visit me on my court dates and bring food and messages, etc. Mum gave him £50, and I never saw him again either; your faith in humanity waves, especially when cheated by a man of faith!

When you realise you're trapped in a spiral, it's often too late.

Emile was out on parole for three months, and he returned in late February with a few bits I had asked him for, like books and an umbrella for the July – September monsoons. He also brought a pen drive full of English songs as the superintendent had allowed a building to be used as a sort of DJ area where one prisoner would play requested songs between 12 pm – 1 pm over the tannoy system. To hear a Bob Marley or an Oasis song, any English song after so long, was like, well, "Music to my ears." I was also receiving the odd newspaper and football magazine from PA, along with word Searches/crossword puzzles, etc., from my family and friends so that I could relieve the boredom slightly. I had also started to receive a lot of letters from Emma and Sarah, two girls who became good future friends.

In March 2015, most newspapers were reporting of the conviction of Ravi Punjabi, who was a close associate of the underworld gangster Ravi Pujari. He was brought into 6 no. circle and placed in a cell three down from me. They were going to put him in the Anda Barrack as he was high profile, but he had already paid the officers on entry to be placed into a separate cell. He had travelled to London and was western educated, so we would relate to songs, movies, and western culture and eventually become mates.

Wherever you go, make friends.

Over the following months, we would walk and chat through the day; it was a relief to have someone to converse with, as Emile was working in the office area most of the day. He managed to arrange a mobile after a week, but he was reluctant to let me use it as he was contacting Pujari, who was in Australia and one of the most wanted men in India. He would text Mum for me, so I was receiving messages from home. In June, he got another phone and gave me the old one with a sim card. Finally, I was back in contact with home. Obviously, hiding the phone was my biggest issue, and I was more concerned with losing my separate cell if caught than the beating or any other punishment. Ravi had managed to get a type of chisel from the work areas, and we used this to break the concrete floor at the back of my cell. Half an inch down was soil, so I made a "10 cigarette box" size type of hole and tunnelled across approximately 10cm. This would give me the room to store batteries for the phone too. I would wrap the phone in plastic and tie it with string leaving a long length so I could push it further along and fish it out when needed. Ravi also got a guard to bring in something called M-Seal; it was like 2 different coloured lumps of plasticine compound, which, when mixed together and moulded, would harden after a couple of hours. With this, I made a rectangular lid to sit in place of the missing concrete. Once the phone and batteries were in place, I would seal the gaps with soap and then sprinkle dry cement on top, it was a brilliant hiding place, and I was a lot more comfortable holding on to the phone. I was back in contact with home at last.

It was over 18 months now since I had applied to the high court, so I resent an application again, requesting that my trial be heard expeditiously. The reason I stated this was that I was a foreign national, and my transfer agreement would not be possible until trial completion. Mum was also very ill; she had angina, shingles, and agoraphobia, which I had also listed in my application. I received the same reply, i.e., my case would be expedited!

It becomes very difficult for the family of the prisoner, too; they suffer, wait, and make every possible effort to see their loved ones out of prison. The suffering and anguish after repeated lies and disappointments. Knowing how my family was suffering hurt the most. I wanted it to end soon, so I could end their hurt. August came around with the news of my second grandchild, Millie-Rose; I was over the moon—a girl and a boy. It was also bittersweet, as it was another family celebration I would miss. During such times, loneliness would hit hard, and homesickness used to crawl inside me.

Just before Christmas that year, Mum and Alf came with the Embassy for a visit. I already told Mum to bring me a load of goodies and a few large Cadbury chocolate bars to give the guards to use as a bribe to help pass my things. It was a good visit, and we got 90 minutes to hold hands, hug, and chat. I discussed my case and how Taraq was telling us the same things: "It's on the board", "Yours should be soon", etc. etc. We decided to move forward, so we would have to change our lawyer and start looking at other options. Mum had brought three full carrier bags of books, clothes, and edible items, and at the end of the visit, the guard started to do his check. Straightaway I got "not allowed", but Mum jumped up and started giving the chocolate bars to officers and guards. They all looked shocked at this little Ninja bouncing about with chocolate. It worked, though, because I got 90% of the items in.

Your family is all that you have in times of despair and distress.

Chapter Seventeen

We had a new superintendent, and he was here to change things for the better. In January 2017, cricket matches, volleyball matches, and chess/carom competitions were organised against each barrack. It was an opportunity to get out of your area for a wander and catch up with people. He also started yoga, there was a type of stone area with a raised platform used for various entertainment on festivals, and he allocated use of this area from 7:15 am to 9:15 am. Every day the superintendents would do rounds along with all the officers; for example, barracks 1 and 2 would be inspected on Mondays and subsequent areas on other days. You basically had to fold all of your bedding and items into the bags and then cover them with a sheet. On your barrack round day, you could make a request or complaint, although complaints were often met with a whack of the bamboo.

My daily exercise routine was yoga and then some weights for an hour. We would get someone to make dumbbells with a six-inch wooden pole and put nails on each end. Then, with some clay mixed with the hair from coconuts, it is shaped into blocks. The end of the pole is pushed in, and once the clay hardens, you have a dumbbell. The bigger the block, the heavier the weight.

My friend Rueban, who I was on the road with and convicted around the same time, was still in 1 no. circle. I would always meet him at the church gathering on Sundays and would go and see him whenever I had the chance. This particular day, as I went in 1 no. circle, various prisoners came up to me, saying, "Rueban's gone mad" or "something wrong". When I saw him sitting there with this glazed expression, I knew I had to try and get him in my area, get his head right again! To see such a lively guy– an intelligent man like him lose his mind was heart-breaking.

I sat him down and told him my intentions, but he was looking at me with suspicion like I had an ulterior motive. I went ahead over the next few days of making an application to the superintendent stating the reasons why he would be better within 6 no. circle with friends. Rueban wanted a separate cell, but because of his mindset, there was no way they would sanction it because of the risk of suicide. They agreed he could stay in 2 no. barrack, and I arranged for him to be in a handi/group with some friends. When the day came to move, he was so suspicious of me that it pained me to watch. Eventually, I got him there, but he had to transfer to the hospital after a week to get treatment. I realised then that the brain is a powerful muscle, and it is a very fine line between sanity and insanity.

The months went by in 2016, but the prison had become very strict as there had been a murder inside. It also became a lot stricter because one idiot had been filmed heating food and smoking weed inside the Anda barrack. He then went on parole and gave the video to the media. It was all over the TV, news, and in the papers. The three guards who used to bring batteries in for me had all been suspended, and no other guards were interested. They had all been warned a case would be put on them if anything was smuggled in.

I really excelled at yoga and was actually teaching the other prisoners most days. It was in a mixture of English, Hindi, and Marathi, so everyone understood; I was quite fluent by now. It really helped me with my flexibility, but most of all, the "Peace of mind" it created was fantastic.

In November 2016, my son Kyle and Daughter-in-law Chantelle gave birth to my 3rd grandchild Autumn-Ivy. I was a triple grandad but had only seen photos. I longed to hear them call me grandad and hold them. It had been seven years since I had been incarcerated, and in hindsight, I wondered if I had made the right decision to challenge my conviction. If I had put in my transfer papers, I would have spent the last two years in an English prison and be out in six months' time. This would have meant I was guilty, but I still believed I had made the right choice to prove my innocence.

In January and February of 2017, Mum contacted a barrister in Birmingham who was of Indian descent and whose mother lived in Mumbai. It was exciting news; all the family was telling me how my plight would be on the news and to the foreign secretary and how they were confident he would get me a new lawyer and get me out. I was told he travelled to India every couple of months and so he would pay for his own flights, etc., and the costs would be minimal.

I got the visit in March; He had paid approximately £200 to the superintendent as a bribe, and the visit took place in the offices. He brought along with him a lawyer from Mumbai and a local lawyer from Kolhapur. It was good to hear an English voice and especially the enthusiasm telling me how he was going to get me out. He was also raging at the severity of the sentence. How can one man decide if you're guilty or not for a medicinal drug? I told him that this is India, and it has its own laws. I got a lift from the visit, "I am going to get you out", he promised!

Over the next couple of months, he travelled to India and contacted a few lawyers. He told my family he could get me the best lawyer, and this lawyer would normally charge £200k. He represents all the big actors. I knew who he was; in India, it's all about the "face Value" and the "reputation" of lawyers, and that's why the judges will be more agreeable or lenient. He wanted £40k, and my mum was talking about re-mortgaging her house to raise the money; she was at her wit's end, and people were saying they would probably never see me again! These big criminal lawyers know nothing about NDPS cases, though all they would do is use some of that money to pay for Taraq Sayed to attend high court. When the Birmingham lawyer came over, he needed all the paperwork relating to my case and managed to eventually get everything from Taraq.

The Birmingham outfit was in the state of opening another office in Manchester and, in May, organised a meeting at the Hilton. No more tension. My mum and dad and their partners, along with a few other family members and friends, attended, along with the mayor, local MP, and media representatives. Looking back, it was all for promoting these new offices. He was not interested in my situation really, maybe initially, but after realising he couldn't get me released, it was all about the No. 5 Chambers, their new Building/Business. One positive thing to come out of this was that we were only out of pocket by £1500. The next thing was that I finally had all my papers from Taraq and could engage a new lawyer. There was only one other name who was an expert in NDPS and whose fees were reasonable. In around August 2017, I got Ayaz Khan on to my case; he had pursued the paperwork and was confident he would get me an acquittal within 3 months, and all for £2500. Things seemed to be looking up again.

My family spoke with Ayaz over the following months. My case was on the board and in the top 20 to be heard. I was allocated a division bench as my sentence exceeded ten years, which meant I would have two judges. In the meantime, Ravi had managed to get his phone batteries charged within the prison. At night the watchmen inside the barrack would charge it via the television. Again, it was a precarious situation because informers and watchmen would be beaten if they were caught. In July, all of my batteries were dead, no one was charging within the jail, and no guards were bringing anything in. I wasn't using the sim card I had gotten from Ravi, so he asked if he could use it till I got a battery. When I did sort one and asked for the sim back, he told me he had broken it because of conversations with Pujari. He was an international Gangster, and one thing about India is that they capture many criminals via phone conversations. Santosh would never speak because of the voice recognition. Ravi said he would arrange for me another sim, but it never came; like most in India, he was talking lies. I fell out with him; that was my lifeline, and I told him so; I also told him to stay out of my way because I wanted to beat him so badly. His excuse was that his bail was happening, and nothing should compromise it, and he reckoned it had cost him two crores, or approximately £200,000. Another letdown, another liar!

In August, there was a huge gang brought into Kolhapur. There were over 120 men in the case based in Pune prison, but they had transferred the boss and 34 others to split them slightly. Mane company they were called, Mane was the main man. Not much different from a military setup came—his lieutenants, 2nd and 3rd in command, and the accountant who organised the money, etc., made up an organised team, and that was why they were under the MCOCA act, which was basically organised crime where bail was not possible. Obviously, these 35 men should all be separated, but money, power talks, and the authorities agreed on situating them all in their own barracks, and that would be in 6 no. circle.

So, what happened was all the workers from the barracks of 6 no. were removed to the B/C barracks, which were basically at the side of the kitchens, and the day/night workers would alternate and sleep in one barrack. So, all of Mane's company moved in straightaway; they played cards, and the bosses blatantly used phones. A couple of the lads spoke good English, and we became quite friendly. The boss had got himself a separate cell after a month. At one lunchtime lock-in, a guard came and opened my cell and said Mane wanted me. So, I got to go to his cell; six other high-ranking members were in there, sitting in a circle. They had a bottle of Tequila, sliced lemon, and seven champagne-type plastic flute glasses. They wanted me to show them how to drink it. I was still amazed at how they had gotten it all in. So, I proceeded to show them with salt on hand, lick it, neck the Tequila, and eat the lemon. An hour later and six drinks down, I went back to my cell. Now, this was a Sunday, and for lunch, they gave you "*Khadi*", which was a milk-based curry. That was where I made the mistake of eating this with a glass of milk; I was ill for two days with fluids coming out of every orifice, so much for English being drinkers, I was teased for days.

Ravi went out on bail in October after a total of 5 and a half years of a 10-year sentence; money and connections can work. All Mane people were charging batteries at night, the authorities knew what was going on, and it didn't help that certain prisoners were coming to 6 no. every day to make calls. As you walked around the barracks now, there would be 3 or 4 using phones, and my area had now become known as Dubai for all the luxuries. I needed batteries charging, so reluctantly, I told the others I had a phone, not something I wanted to do because loose lips sink ships and Indians are like women for gossiping.

The last couple of months of 2017 were a total nightmare. The Dubai area was getting checks 3-4 times a week; they would normally come before opening or after closing time and search while you were present. Not anymore; they were filing us all out and spending an hour at a time intensely searching, breaking floors and walls, and digging up outside. It was working; however, if you were with the guards while a search was happening, you could distract them or offer some money if an illegal item was found. Things were changing, and they were finding two or three mobiles a week; there was a lot of information going on!

Just before Christmas of 2017, three officers and three guards came to my cell after lock-in. I knew they had received information, and I sat outside while they smashed all my floors in. The mobile was found, and also the sim card, which I used to put behind the grout in a small tiled area. My cell was destroyed, and I had to sleep in the barrack until the next morning. I would lose my separate cell and maybe get a beating, but the thing that hurt most was that the contact with my family would be gone again.

Chapter Eighteen

They wouldn't open my cell the next morning; I would have to go and see the superintendent for my punishment. The sim card was my downfall, as they knew I had used the mobile. I got along with 90% of the authorities, and we had mutual respect for each other. Superintendent Jadwar was also firm but fair.

As I walked into his office, I asked Jadwar, "Why have the guards trashed my cell and belongings"?

"A mobile phone was found, a sim card, and a charger underground", he said.

"Well, I know nothing about it", I said. I wasn't completely lying, as I didn't know there was a charger". "As I am a foreign national, it would not look good for the prison if it was exposed."

He said, "If you compromise with me, I will compromise with you."

He was basically saying, "don't tell the embassy or anyone."

I agreed, but I told him I wanted another separate in 6n°. All my friends were there, and I had settled in that cell for the last two and a half years. He wouldn't agree, but I said I could have a separate in 8n°; there were 4 in there used as punishment.

I said, "My case is on board. I will be acquitted any time. Please, don't start moving me now. I've adjusted and am content in 6n°circle."

Well, he wasn't listening to me at all, so I had to get all my belongings and move there at the lock-in. I had not been in 8n° circle since my arrival here in 2013, when it was used mainly for newly convicted prisoners. Now, it housed mainly the workers who worked in the fields or wood/metal departments, so it was quite empty for most of the day. There were barracks in there with four separate cells. It was a large area, with the barracks completing a type of circle with how they were situated. I was well-known throughout the prison now since I was the only English man there. So, I would spend an hour walking with a few working lads, and once they left, I would do my exercise. I was still attending yoga every morning, and the exercise would take me past 10 a.m., leaving one and a half hours till the next lock-in. Playing cards or any type of betting was not allowed, but I had asked the embassy to bring me dominoes on their 3-monthly visit on Christmas this time. However, after a lot of arguing and persuasion, I was allowed to receive dominoes from them. This game helped me pass many mundane hours.

It was now 2018, and Ayaz had still not gotten me an acquittal as promised. As I had no phone again, I resent an application to the DIG and requested the embassy to speak to her. I wanted to call home twice a month. There was now a provision in place for Indian prisoners for more than a year to make a call twice a month. The person who they wished to phone was first verified by the police, and once in place, they got 5-8 minutes twice a month. So, in my application, I asked for the same—what is good enough for them should be for me too.

In February, a lad was brought in from Arthur Road who had been convicted of 10 years. His name was Rohit, and he was from Himachal Pradesh. A cooler Northern part of India in the Himalayas. It was a relief to have someone to speak English to again, and he brought me news of Arthur Road and how my London mate, Bill, was doing; his trial was still ongoing after six years. So, I got into a routine in my new area where after exercise was done, we would play dominoes for an hour. Between 3 p.m. and 5 p.m., we would have a walk and play games; it was less stressful here because searches were less frequent, and most prisoners were working during the day, which meant basically, they were poor and couldn't afford mobiles or other prohibited things.

So, the first couple of months in my new area passed very slowly until Rohit arrived. Emile had actually finished a total of 8 years and two months, had accrued some remission, and was released. It feels lonelier when a close friend leaves, and you're still there. I was ecstatic for Emile; don't get me wrong, but it still pained me to know that convicted murderers could get remission for good behaviour, yet it was not available for drug cases. Still, he was a good man, and I was happy that he was finally free.

Over May and June, many convicted prisoners were sent to Kolhapur despite the fact that the prison was already overcrowded, and so were others in Maharashtra. As a result, everyone in the barracks just had to live with even less space and cramped conditions. One morning, a lad named Alishan came to my cell, who had just been sent to Kolhapur with a 10-year sentence from Arthur Road. He was very western educated and had even visited London and Blackpool. He was friends with Bill in Arthur Road and brought some news about him and his general life there. I felt so good again to connect with someone who understood you and your life. I knew things would be harder for him in jail, same as myself. What I mean by this is "you can't miss what you've never had", and nearly all of the prisoners had never travelled or had luxuries, so I believe it was harder for the ones who had.

Over the next couple of months, it was the same routine: walk, exercise, play, and then do it all again in the afternoon. Rohit had started working in the carpentry area most of the day, so it was good to have Alishan there. He was paying the officer in charge of 8n° at that time, and then the superintendent, on a round one day, told him to change the circle since 8n° was only for the workers.

So, I found it harder to pass the days again. I had other Indian friends, of course, but it's not the same as conversing in "Hinglish". During the embassy's 3-monthly visits in August, I finally received some good news. Over the previous years, I had constantly been fighting for phone calls on numerous occasions via applications, and it had somehow been sanctioned. It was the first time in India that I believed a foreigner had this opportunity. They had a coin box telephone for the Indian prisoners, but obviously, that option was not available for me, so it was agreed I could use the superintendent's phone for video calling every 15 days. The embassy had to arrange with the British police to verify it would be my mum's mobile I was phoning. We also had to make a 3-way conversation where Navaz from the embassy would also be present, a conference call if you like. That first call was incredible. To see and speak with my mum and knowing I'd get another opportunity in 15 days to do it again was a huge relief for all of us.

The call time was usually around 12 p.m., once all the prisoners were locked in. Unfortunately, as India is approximately five hours ahead, Mum had to be awake early to take the calls. My son, Kyle, and my grandson, Kai, were there the weeks after too, and I spoke with them. I had completed nearly nine years, but I was so happy and content being able to now have that contact with the family so we could reassure each other. Obviously, my main questions were about how everyone was, but a close second was, "What's happening in my appeal?"

In September, my case was finally on the board before a division bench of two judges. As my sentence was ten years consecutively, it was effectively a 20-year sentence, and anything more than ten years of conviction was to be heard by a division bench of two or more judges. Two judges effectively agreed the two lots of ten years should be made concurrent to a sentence of ten. Then, they passed it down to a single judge bench as Indian law states they couldn't run the appeal now it was ten years. It is typical to make the rules as they go in this country. On the bright side, something had finally happened. The division bench had also given a ruling that it must be heard within a 3-month period. I could be home for Christmas 2018. I was just hoping and praying every day.

Chapter Nineteen

There was an exciting buzz within my family and friends again. We all just hoped and prayed that our ordeal would finally come to an end. I obviously wanted an acquittal; I was innocent and had made it this far for nothing, but now, I was tired. Even if I knew I would have to finish the year as a guilty man, then so be it. All I wanted was a decision.

The next few months went by slowly. Rohit had started working, so the days dragged by, trying to pass my time. Ayaz had written to me at the prison, which is unheard of for lawyers in India. He basically told me that the judge in front of whom my appeal was heard was not very liberal and usually sided with the prosecution, meaning no acquittal. He advised all the family and me to wait a few months until this judge was changed and that it was a common practice every 3-6 months in the high court. After spending so long here, it was not worth the gamble. The word around the prison was that a woman judge named 'Sadhana Jadhav' would soon be sitting in the NDPS cases courtroom. She had a reputation for being a nice judge, with so many acquittals in NDPS. So, it was agreed that we would be patient and the wait wouldn't be too long.

As I said, leading up to the Christmas of 2018/19 was tiring, waiting for the judge to change and mainly conversing in 'Hinglish' most days. In December, a few lads were transferred to my area from other barracks for fighting. I knew them all; over time, you get to know who's who around the prison. They weren't gangsters, but they were respected by the other prisoners. I started them jogging and exercising with me in the mornings after yoga, and I had a few new domino partners. Christmas came and went as usual. The sponge cake and the chicken being recooked to last four or five days. The stark truth was that this was my tenth Christmas in India, and I didn't want to celebrate it!

Into January 2019, as I mentioned, I had a few new friends in my area, and these lads liked a 'smoke'. As there were a lot of informants, I used to keep a lookout or use somebody to watch for the guards whilst they smoked. You get ganja in India, which is apparently very cheap on the outside, but the guards brought it in at inflated prices. They also smoke it in a chillum, which is a type of conical-shaped clay pipe that is carved out. The preparation for smoking the chillum is also a long, drawn-out process, but this wasn't an issue as we had plenty of time. So basically, the people who were smoking all sat crossed-legged in a circle. One person would do the mix. This involved removing all the seeds from the ganja first, mixing the remainder in with the tobacco, and using a palm and a thumb on the opposite hand to make it really fine, like dust. There would be a small stone at the bottom of the chillum to act as a filter to stop the mix from coming through. The lad that was starting to light it or the 'shooter' would continually riff until the chillum pipe was alight and inhale a load before passing it to the next man. The amount of 'pulls' or 'blasts' depended on the number of ganja cigarettes that were in the mix.

It was a Sunday, and my area was full of all the workers and barbers. I was sitting, looking through a couple of magazines, when five of the lads came into my separate cell and asked if they could make a chillum. They arranged for a lookout, and all sat down and made a big mix. One chillum had been smoked, and the second was made and ready to light up when the circle officer and a guard came rushing in. After a quick search, they found the chillum, and then the guard started hitting everyone with his bamboo stick. He was abusing us all in Marathi, calling us all bastards and mother/sister fuckers while hitting our legs and arms. We were all standing at this point, and he was turning to each one of us individually. When he got to me, I was thinking, '*he won't hit me because I'm a foreigner and a British one, to add!*' He stood in front of me and slapped my face; it was a shock, and I really had to stop myself from a reaction punch. I then got a whack across my calves till he moved on to the next man. I wished this guard would have punched me rather than a slap, it was humiliating, and I really wanted to retaliate. If I did, I knew the beating and the aftermath would be so much worse, so I had to bite my tongue.

After the guard got tired of beating everybody and cleared us out of the cell, another 3 guards came to do a search. They ransacked everything; sugar and other things were thrown on the floor with my clothes. No need to be so excessive! They also found a '*kapne*', which is a piece of metal fashioned into a blade that I used for cutting fruits and things. They also found my homemade shaving stick made from a pen with a blade melted into it. I was sent to sleep in one of the barracks that night and would have to see the superintendent the next day!

After the circle roundabout on Monday, we were all called out to the Mandal, where all the officers sat. The superintendent, senior superintendent, and five 3-star officers were sitting behind a long table. Others and I were all in there together, so I knew we wouldn't get a second beating; for that, they only called us in separately. They each asked a few questions and passed a few snide comments. The superintendent then 'circled everyone out', meaning he gave each of us new areas to move into. When he told me to go to 3n° circle, which I knew had no separate cells, I obviously had to protest; I said, "I will be acquitted anytime soon. Please, don't put me in the barrack; I can't adjust here. After six years of staying alone, I will end up on a murder charge". He eventually allowed me to move back to 6n° separate, and I was on the move again.

Chapter Twenty

It wasn't the same as before in 6N° Circle. The people had changed along with the atmosphere. The two barracks in there now house minors under 20 years of age, and 6/2N° was now used as an after barrack. The barrack was used for new arrivals and prisoners who had arrived late from the court, etc., so there were no belongings. It felt empty and bare, and the barrack 6/1 was full of young kids! There was a prisoner in one of the other separates, he was an ex-lawyer who had served close to 18 years for murder, and he spoke good English. There were also five policemen and a civilian in the cells, accused of murdering a man by torture while in their custody. I settled in and adjusted, but I knew the time would be my Achilles' heel; it wouldn't pass quickly with the people I was with.

I was still getting my video call every 14-20 days, and that kept me going along with exercise and games. The gossip around the prison in early February 2019 was that Sadhna Jadhav had been transferred to the NDPS courtroom within the high court, and mum confirmed this on a call. Ayaz had said that he was filing an application straight away before her to start arguments for the appeal. It seemed that, finally, something was going right for me.

When I next had contact with my mum, she told me that Ayaz had said the judge had agreed to start the arguments within six weeks; it was a huge relief; as you can imagine, the following six weeks of waiting were horrendous, hoping and praying for the appeal to start. I always tried to look at the positives, but I had that many orders from judges stating the appeal must start within a certain time frame and weren't honoured. I was more of a pessimist than an optimist now! I had resigned to "hoping for the best, expecting the worst". I felt like I had been kicked in the testicles, and many times I now had four tonsils.

If I wasn't acquitted, I would have to complete my sentence and pay the approximate £4000 fine. The problem was though I was innocent, I wanted my freedom, and with the tens of thousands we had already spent, we couldn't really afford the fine. I say that, but mum and the family would have got the amount together rather than me serving an extra four years.

It was a very anxious period for me. The next call I got was in April. Mum told me that the arguments from Ayaz and the persecution were completed, and all we had to do was wait for the judge's decision. Normally, with appeals, the judge will pass judgment / give a verdict within a 14-day period. Mum also told me that she had been informed by Ayaz that the judge had also promised to give the verdict before the month ends. I was 36 years old when I came to India, and it was my 46th birthday on May 2nd. Could I be celebrating this one at home with my family and friends? I felt nervous and sick, mixed with hope and excitement.

Each day that passed felt like a week! When a prisoner is released, their name is shouted over the Tannoy system to collect their metal plate and bowl, and bedding and take it to the main gate.

Until I had my next call home, I had heard nothing. Why was the verdict not been given yet?! Mum had reassured me and said Ayaz told her it would definitely be soon. "It only antagonises the judge if you push them, so just be patient". I was fed up with being patient and sick of hearing the same things.

It never happened before my birthday, it never happened in May, and it went into June with still no verdict; it was a horrendous time! Every hour of every day, listening for my name to be called. All in all, it took the judge three months from closing arguments to do her summing up and verdict.

It was Wednesday, July 7th, when I was called to the superintendent's office. I just hoped he had some good news for me. As I walked in, I just knew he was smiling from ear to ear and stood up with his hand and offered to shake mine. I honestly really don't know how I felt at that moment, there were too many emotions, but most of all, I felt relief. It was like this weight that had burdened me for nearly ten years had suddenly gone. I wasn't excited and jumping for joy; the Euphoria had been overpowered by the sheer sense of relief

The superintendent, Jadwar Sahib, went on to tell me that there were conditions alongside the acquittal. One of these was that I could not remain in India and must be deported within ten days. Unbeknownst at the time, this order from the judge would be a big blessing for me. I had a good rapport with the superintendent, so he phoned Rey in Mumbai and let me speak for five minutes. We had already earlier discussed and pre-planned what we were going to do. I knew of prisoners acquitted in Kolhapur who had to wait up to six weeks for release because the paperwork had not arrived. Once you have been acquitted by the high court, the papers then go to the session court. A few stamps, seals, and signatures, and it is all completed. So, how it takes so long to reach the prison, I will never know. Everything was in place; Rey would collect all the papers and do the needful from the high court to the session. My family had sent money for him to have a car and a driver, too; they would have to leave Mumbai at midnight for the 11-hour drive.

Chapter Twenty-One

I walked back to my circle from the office with a million thoughts and emotions in my head. I realised the date when the first time I was convicted on July 7th, 2013, and now, I was being acquitted on July 7th 2019, exactly six years to the day. I had served a total of nine years and eight months! I felt proud that I had survived mentally and physically, but I was on autopilot. I wouldn't take anything for gospel until I had placed both my feet on British soil.

A few prisoners asked, "Kya Hua" - "What happened"? on the walk back. The majority of the prisoners knew I was awaiting a verdict, and they were all overjoyed for me. I told all the lads in my area, then went and told Reuban, who was still in the hospital area; his mental health was still bad, and he was a shadow of the man I first met in 2009. I went to all the different areas that afternoon to tell a few African and Indian lads my news; everyone asked, "Can I have your towel"? Or some other item like clothes.

My name was called at 11:30 a.m. the next day. When I got to the office, Rey was there with all the paperwork. I walked in and gave him a man hug, and he broke down crying; bless him; He had lived through my ordeal along with my family, so I could understand his emotion. He had even started calling my mum his mum, and my family loved him for all of his help and support over the years.

"All of my belongings are packed", I told Jadwar Sahir in Hindi. "Can I get them and leave now?" I only had to look at his face to know there was some problem.

"The order from the judge says you must be deported, so I have spoken to the customs officer in charge, and they have said they will come and take you to a detention centre until they can put you on a flight", Jadwar said.

All my plans to go to Rey's and try and bring myself back to reality until I had travelled home were gone.

"So, when will they arrive"? I asked.

"I will look into it and make some calls", he said.

I was fuming! I had proven my innocence and was free now but still incarcerated.

I said my goodbyes to Rey, and somehow I managed to get through that afternoon and evening. As the hours passed by on Friday morning with still no news, I'd had enough. At lunch-lock-in, I went to see Jadwar and asked, "Sir, what's happening?"

"Well, it's complicated because we have never had an order for deportation, so nobody seems to know the procedure". It was the last straw for me.

"I am legally free and being detained against my will, so I am just going to walk out now. Can you stop me?" I asked just to make sure, "The tower guards won't shoot at me, will they?"

He could see my anguish and desperation; I had spent far too long in an alien country!

"Please, do not create a fuss, Barry. I will try to find another way", he said.

After a few calls, he arranged for me to be taken to Mumbai to be handed over to the customs there. One officer would go with me, he said, and hand me over to the customs when we arrived. I had saved over £80 over the past six years from my PPC account. I collected this and said all my goodbyes. Outside the prison, we both jumped on the back of his motorbike; it was quite surreal and bizarre, really, but I felt free at last. We grabbed a snack from a street vendor and parked the bike in the bus stand car park, and proceeded to get a coach to Pune.

The guard was only young, around 28, but he was a decent lad. His friend lived in Mumbai, so we would meet up with him. Rey had bought us some whiskey for them after him mithering me; everything was at my expense, including his travel. We arrived at the Pune bus station around 8 p.m., then got in a "shared taxi" to Mumbai, arriving at 1:30 p.m., met up with the guard's friend and Rey, and then headed to Rey's place. Rey had met a woman from NE India a few years earlier, and they had a newborn baby together. It was only two tiny rooms, and the guard and his mate were supposed to be staying as well. They actually expected to have a party, but it was the last thing I wanted. The guard and his friend eventually left around 2 a.m. on a promise I would meet him at Bandra train station by 9 a.m. the next day.

He had to hand me over. "Please, be there because I will lose my job", he said.

The train system in Mumbai is on another level. The crowds of humans just carry you along, and the sights, sounds, and smells all hit you at once, overloading the senses. We made our way to the foreign office in central Mumbai only to realise it was the "Second Saturday" in India, the second and fourth Saturday of each month was a non-working day, and all government buildings were closed.

The guard then said to me, "I need to go back to Kolhapur, so you will have to come and travel back on Monday with me".

I told him, "You have got no chance of me doing".

He phoned Jadwar at the prison. Jadwar instructed him to contact a 3-star officer who worked at Byculla women's prison in Mumbai, and we headed there. I knew the officer from earlier, and he was alright. He took the paper and said, "You can meet me at the foreign office on Monday at 10 p.m." As I was sitting, waiting for all documents to be sorted, a prison van drove into the car park. "Baz, Baz!" I heard. It was only Bill, my London friend from Arthur Road. I was buzzing, I even tried jumping in the back of the van to hug him, but he didn't look the same. Prison life was taking its toll on him!

Chapter Twenty-Two

My mum booked me a flight to Manchester via a stop in Dubai later that night. We decided to book it for the following Saturday, as I wanted a little time to reconnect with the world. I had to get used to all these big new phones with touchscreens and other things. I wanted to do a bit of shopping and, maybe, get my teeth whitened. Rey had his daughter now all week because his wife had to go to work, so I had to navigate the trains myself! I managed to find my way to the customer's branch, where I gave them the release papers. I then had to travel to the British embassy offices, probably another 20 miles on the other side of the city. When I arrived, Navaz and a couple of other staff members I had met over the years greeted me. They all genuinely looked ecstatic that I was finally free; maybe, it was just relief on Navaz's face because my mum would now stop constantly phoning and harassing her about me. The embassy had helped me in a lot of ways, but they had also told a lot of lies, so my mum constantly berated them.

I was in the embassy offices until around 6 p.m. All my details were uploaded with the flight details printed on my EFD (Electronic Flight

Document). Rey had cooked me a nice meal of prawns and some other bits he had bought from the market when I arrived back. I felt a bit more at ease now that everything was sorted, so I bought a few beers too.

The seafood didn't agree with me, and I was up and down all night vomiting, so I wasn't feeling my best when Ayaz phoned, and I certainly wasn't prepared.

"Barry, get yourself down to the High Court today by 2 p.m. because the prosecution is filing an order before the judge to keep you here for six months so they can have time to appeal against your acquittal in the supreme court".

Why is this happening? I am not a bad person, so why is God still punishing my loved ones and me? I felt sick, and my heart was literally in my mouth, so close I could touch it, but again something to ruin our happiness; it was a living nightmare and a reoccurring one.

I headed to the train station again at 1 p.m. I was getting adept at travelling to central Mumbai. I met Ayaz and his assistant outside the courtroom.

"How can they do this now? There is an order for me to be deported."

Ayaz said, "It won't stick. They are just trying it on".

I told Ayaz, "Tell the judge that if the prosecution wants me to stay in India, they should provide me with accommodation, clothing, and food".

How could I support myself after everything over the last nine years and eight months? I was broken. We stood at the back of the courtroom, and I had to go to the toilet around 4.30 p.m. As I walked back towards the door, Ayaz was already standing outside with his assistants.

"Be back here, same time tomorrow", he said. "The judge has adjourned it till then".

He went on to tell me he had told the judge about the living expenses and the deportation order and that I had already had my flight booked for Saturday evening. I had a million questions, but Ayaz was off to another courtroom. I had no choice but to return the following day around the same time!

It was a Thursday now, and I had two days to do everything in my power to get out of this hell hole of a country. When I got to court, nobody was around, so I phoned Ayaz. He said, "Did Sartaj, my assistant, not tell you that the judge was busy, so he has postponed the hearing until tomorrow"?

I was fuming; the travel cost wasn't expensive, but it was a harrowing journey, and I hated doing it. There were a million thoughts running through my head. Friday was the last court day until Monday. I just felt deflated, I was still on autopilot, but my resolve was breaking.

Groundhog Day on Friday had me back at the court. I arrived 5 minutes later, and the judge had already pronounced his decision. Ayaz told me the judge had offered the prosecution a 3-month maximum time frame to submit their appeal before the supreme court. In that period, he told me that they would also have to provide living expenses, and that was the clincher for me, I believe. All I needed from the customs officers was a NOC (No Objection Certificate) so that I could leave the country. What they wanted from me was a guarantor, somebody to vouch that I would return to India in the event of a re-trial. I was willing to do virtually anything right then to get that NOC Ayaz told me Navaz from the embassy could sign as she has known me now for more than five years.

I returned to Rey's that Friday. I was a little more hopeful, but with my new motto that I now had ingrained, "Hope for the best, prepare for the worst". I was in phone contact with Navaz up until 8 p.m. That evening, she had been speaking to various important colleagues, and because India is a commonwealth country and has an embassy and not a consulate, it would be illegal for them to act as a guarantor for me. Navaz was also in contact with the customs officer in charge, and after a lot of back and forth, he had agreed for a notary to be completed to act as a guarantor. A notary is taken by a licensed person who uses a few seals and stamps on documents to verify who you are, etc. I didn't understand the whole point, which was to use a contact who has known you, not a random person, but I wasn't about to argue. I spoke to Ayaz, and he told me to meet up with Sartaj at a particular building in Mumbai at 9 a.m. in the morning to arrange everything.

Chapter Twenty-Three

It was the same process again on Saturday morning. I arrived in Mumbai around 9 AM and met with Sartaj. Eventually, we found the Notary offices and did the needful work; it cost me less than ten sterling. Around 10:30 AM, I made my way back to the foreign office with new instructions to be added to the paperwork. This all took till around 1 PM to complete. After that, I made my way to the customs office only to have to wait till 3 PM for the officer, but it didn't matter as I finally had the golden ticket. The N.O.C. I was ready to fly out of the country. I was still on autopilot and taking nothing for granted, but the tension had lifted considerably. Could I finally be going home?

I was in good spirits back at Rey's apartment. We all were, including all my family and friends, over the phone. The mobile phone I bought rang at 11 PM. I looked at the caller I.D., and it was Navaz. I instantly got that sinking feeling; my flight was only hours away.

"Hello, Navaz," I said, half laughing, "don't you be giving me any bad news!"

"Barry, I'm really sorry," she stated. "I have been informed that the Emirates flight you have booked will need to be changed." She then continued to tell me I would need to book a direct flight home. Emirates had informed her that on arrival to Dubai, the immigration there would send me straight back to India on the next available flight.

I couldn't believe it. Did I have a curse over me or something? Can I get another flight? What if they arrest me again? My head was spinning with questions.

Navaz and the embassy staff all wanted me back home with my family as much as I wanted to be back, and Navaz agreed to open the embassy for me on a Sunday morning. I phoned mum and told her all the bad news. I felt for the family as they had hired a mini-bus to travel to Manchester airport to greet me there. Mum cancelled the flight, and we got a little bit of our money returned to us; the problem we faced now was getting flight availabilities to London. As it was late and India was 5 and a half hours ahead, we decided to try to sleep for a few hours. Mum said she would wake up at 5 AM and phone emirates and look at booking an evening flight direct to Heathrow.

I didn't get much sleep; I just wanted to get out of this hell hole. To be deported by the judge but still be here was ridiculous. I needed this nightmare to end now!

I contacted Navaz, who agreed to open the building and meet me there at 1 PM. Mum and Alf had managed to get me booked on a flight to Heathrow leaving at 4 AM; I would be on English soil again by 10 AM. G.M.T time, hopefully. My son Kyle and one of my best mates, Jonny said they would come and pick me up, so it worked out quite well as they could set off around 5 AM and beat most of the morning traffic. I prayed hard that night and in the morning, too, that nothing else would go wrong, but I wasn't convinced.

I made my way over to a place called "Bandra" to the British embassy and met Navaz around 12.30 PM on Sunday. It took until around 2 PM to update and print out my new flight details on the "Emergency Flight Document (EFD)". We spoke with the customs officer by phone and reassured him that I would meet him at the airport. Navaz would meet "the customs people" with the new EFD and relevant paperwork that afternoon. Even though I had been deported and had also paid for my own flight, they were still worried I would abscond so I could remain in India! I should have actually been in a detention centre, to be fair, but they all knew how desperate I was to return home to my family, so they were lenient with me.

I did a little shopping for new clothes in the afternoon on the way home. I was getting quite adept now navigating my way around Mumbai. The evening went by slowly, and I eventually got in a taxi for the airport with Rey around 12.30 PM. The customs officer kept on phoning me in a panic. The fact was I didn't have to check in and stuff, so I arrived two and a half hours before my flight and not four hours as they had wanted.

I said my goodbyes to Rey. He shed a few tears, he really had come through for me over these past few years, and I was eternally grateful. We had helped him financially here and there, but either way, despite everything, he would have helped us as he had a caring and honest heart. I walked into the terminal and met with the customs man. I still had the cheek to ask if I could get some duty-free goods, " You won't be getting a boarding pass," I was told! We sat in a room with immigration officers stamping all my documents for an hour and waited to board. I told the guy with me to go home. "No!" he said, "I cannot leave until the plane is airborne."

I realised at one point that he was working with another man as he kept making eye contact from afar. My suspicions were confirmed when I went to the toilet, and he followed me like an undercover spy! I mean, I know it was a serious thing, but I was fed up with being treated like an international terrorist criminal...I was an innocent man and made sure I told him my feelings!

I was still on auto-pilot as I got on the plane, and it all still didn't seem real. The head of cabin crew was informed of the situation and was handed all of the paperwork, and she would also be escorting me off the aircraft once all of the other passengers had disembarked.

The 10-hour flight passed by, and I was taken directly to passport control, where I was cleared within 5 minutes or so. Even when I sat on the plane on the runway at Mumbai airport, I was expecting a fleet of police cars screeching on and dragging me back off. So, I finally let out a sigh of relief, it still seemed slightly surreal, but here I was back in my homeland. Now the thing is, I'm a Salford lad or a 'manc' as some would say. But I got on my hands and knees and kissed the floor. London was still a bit like home.

NO MORE TENSION

About the Author

Barry Hulse started writing when he was a student, but he is now a full-time writer. Today, Mr Hulse lives a peaceful, secluded life near Manchester, England. However, he has been through hell and back.

The morning of 21 Nov 2009 brought him a startling turn—a turn he had never thought even in his wildest dreams. As he loved vacationing, he visited Goa, India, in 2009 as he had done before.

He was arrested on the charges of possessing drugs. The officers placed him in an interrogation room and told him that they had seized a package with his details on it three years ago in 2006. They had been looking for him since then. In India, he was put on trial for drug charges, and he had to remain in various prisons there. That period in the Indian prison engulfed a great part of his life.

In this book, you will get to see it all in great detail and how he kept his spirit high during that worst time in his life. So, after coursing through many hardships in his life, Mr Hulse now understands how precious life is and that one should grasp it and live it to the fullest. He has always loved the idea of spreading joy and positivity in the world through his writing.

Barry, or Baz returned home to a grandson & 2 granddaughters. His aim now is to inspire as many individuals as he can through his work, including his grandchildren.

Printed in Great Britain
by Amazon